The Path to Renewal After Collapse:

The Ultimate Guide to Rebuilding a Civilization with Dynamic Practices and Core Principles

(Independent Living Series)

PUBLISHED BY Eagle's Nest Editions

© Copyright 2024 - All rights reserved.

All introductions, analyses, and commentaries contained within this book may not be reproduced, duplicated, or transmitted without direct written permission from the author or the publisher. Under no circumstances will any blame or legal responsibility be held against the publisher or author for any damages, reparation, or monetary loss due to the information contained within this book, either directly or indirectly.

This book is only for personal use. You cannot amend, distribute, sell, use, quote, or paraphrase any part of the introductions, analyses, or commentaries within this book, without the consent of the author or publisher.

Table of contents

Introduction 6

Chapter 1: Surviving the Collapse 12

    1.1 Understanding the Collapse 12

    1.2 Immediate Survival Needs 16

    1.3 Self-Defense and Security 22

    1.4 Forming a Survival Group.. 26

Chapter 2: Establishing Resilient Food Systems for Long-Term Survival 30

    2.1 Adaptive Gardening for Survival 31

    2.2 Foraging and Hunting.. 35

    2.3 Sustainable Animal Practices for a New Era 40

    2.4 Food Preservation Techniques 45

Chapter 3: Building and Maintaining Shelter 50

    3.1 Choosing Locations for Resilient Living............................ 50

    3.2 Basic Construction Techniques 53

    3.3 Advanced Building Techniques 58

    3.4 Maintenance and Repairs 63

Chapter 4: Adapting to a Changing Climate 68

    4.1 Building Resilient Communities Against Climate Shocks . 68

    4.2 Living Sustainably in a Changed Environment.................. 70

    4.3 Harnessing Nature to Mitigate Future Risks..................... 74

    4.4 Preparing for Long-Term Environmental Challenges........ 76

Chapter 5: Water Management and Sanitation 80

5.1 Finding and Purifying Water 80

5.2. Building Water Systems 82

5.3 Waste Management and Sanitation 84

5.4 Community Water Infrastructure 87

Chapter 6: Reestablishing Communication and Transportation 90

6.1 Emergency Communication Systems 90

6.2 Rebuilding Transportation Networks 93

6.3 Signaling for Help 96

6.4 Long-Distance Travel and Exploration 99

Chapter 7: Power and Energy Solutions 102

7.1. Harnessing Solar Energy 102

7.2 Wind and Water Power 105

7.3 Bioenergy and Sustainable Fuels 108

7.4 Energy Storage Solutions 110

7.5 Energy Conservation Strategies 113

Chapter 8: Creating Adaptive Governance and Resilient Societies 118

8.1 Establishing Leadership 118

8.2 Creating Laws and Regulations 121

8.3 Building a Resilient Culture 123

Chapter 9: Health and Medicine in a New World 127

9.1 Building a Community Health System 127

9.2 Traditional and Herbal Medicine 130

9.3 Preventive Healthcare and Hygiene 132

9.4 Emergency Medical Response 136

Chapter 10: Education and Knowledge Preservation 140

10.1 Establishing a Learning Environment 140

10.2 Teaching Practical Skills 142

10.3 Science and Technology for the Future 145

Chapter 11: Reconnecting with Nature 149

11.1 Restoring Natural Ecosystems 149

11.2 Sustainable Agriculture and Permaculture 152

11.3 Preparing for Environmental Challenges 154

Conclusion: The Path Forward: Building a Thriving and Resilient Future 158

Introduction

"In the end, we will remember not the words of our enemies, but the silence of our friends." – Martin Luther King Jr.

This powerful truth strikes at the heart of this book's message. In moments of crisis, it's not the external threats that define our fate, but the choices—both made and unmade—by those we trust and depend on. As you turn these pages, let this quote be more than a reflection; let it be a rallying cry. It calls on you to prepare not just for your own survival, but for the strength of your community, the well-being of your loved ones, and the legacy you'll leave for generations yet to come. The future we rebuild begins with what we choose to do today.

Overview

The second edition of *The Path to Renewal After Collapse* is not just a survival manual; it's your compass for navigating and thriving in a post-collapse world. This book goes beyond stockpiling canned goods and water filters—it's about preparing your mind, honing your skills, and acquiring the knowledge to rebuild a sustainable, resilient society from the ashes. Building on the success of *The Ultimate Guide to Rebuilding a Civilization*, I've expanded this edition to tackle challenges you might not see coming, inspired by feedback from readers like you.

Civilization is a delicate web, held together by threads of economy, environment, and governance. History shows that even the mightiest empires can crumble—whether through internal discord, natural disasters, or external pressures. A societal collapse might feel like a distant possibility, but the truth is, the foundation of modern life is more fragile than we think. A pandemic, an economic meltdown, or a global conflict could disrupt everything we take for granted.

This book is your blueprint for resilience, organized around four pillars critical to navigating uncertainty and rebuilding a thriving community:

- **Survival:** The first, urgent steps—securing essentials like water, food, shelter, and safety in the chaos of collapse.
- **Sustainability:** Building for the long haul, with renewable energy, sustainable agriculture, and systems that outlast the crisis.
- **Independence:** Cultivating the skills and self-reliance needed to break free from failing modern systems.
- **Social Reconstruction:** Reimagining society from the ground up—crafting governance, education, and healthcare systems to rebuild communities that are not just functional, but fair.

This is more than a book; it's a toolkit for hope, grit, and ingenuity when the world as you know it ceases to exist.

The purpose of this book is simple yet ambitious: to give you the ultimate blueprint for rebuilding civilization from the ground up. Whether you're a seasoned survivalist, a curious prepper, a community leader, or just someone passionate about sustainability, this guide is crafted to arm you with the knowledge and strategies needed to rise from the ashes of a societal collapse.

This isn't just about surviving the storm—it's about rebuilding after it passes. From securing life's essentials like water, food, and shelter, to tackling the monumental tasks of establishing governance, rebuilding infrastructure, and creating sustainable systems, this book leaves no stone unturned. It's a step-by-step guide to navigating both the immediate challenges and the long-term vision of starting anew.

You don't need to be an expert to benefit from this guide. It's designed for everyone—from beginners taking their first steps into preparedness to seasoned preppers looking to fill gaps in their plans. This book is for anyone who sees the value of being ready—not just for themselves, but for their loved ones, their communities, and the generations that will inherit the world we leave behind.

The Importance of Historical Lessons

History is a tapestry woven with the rise and fall of civilizations—great societies brought low by a mix of external pressures and internal fragility. The collapse of the Roman Empire, the decline of the Mayan civilization, and the fall of ancient Mesopotamia stand as powerful reminders: no matter how advanced, no society is invincible.

But history doesn't just recount failures—it also tells stories of resilience. From the ashes of catastrophe, many civilizations have rebuilt, often emerging stronger, wiser, and more united. These tales of recovery provide a blueprint for us, offering insights into how to approach the monumental task of rebuilding should our own civilization falter.

This book draws deeply from those lessons of the past. By examining the triggers of collapse—whether environmental, economic, or social—we can anticipate and address similar vulnerabilities in our time. Even more importantly, by studying how societies have risen again, we uncover the principles, strategies, and values that will be critical in shaping a resilient and thriving future. Let history be both a warning and a guide as we prepare for the challenges ahead.

Framework of the Book

This expanded edition features ten chapters—one more than the original—each diving into a crucial element of rebuilding civilization. Designed to take you step-by-step from immediate survival to long-term societal renewal, this book equips you to tackle the challenges of starting over. Here's a sneak peek at what's inside:

1. **Surviving the Collapse:** Learn to identify the signs of societal breakdown, cope with the psychological toll, and secure life's essentials—water, food, shelter, and safety—when chaos strikes.

2. **Establishing a Sustainable Food Supply:** Master the art of growing, foraging, hunting, and preserving food to sustain yourself and your community over the long haul.
3. **Building and Maintaining Shelter:** Discover how to construct durable, resource-efficient shelters, including advanced techniques for sustainable building.
4. **Adapting to a Changing Climate:** Develop strategies to build climate resilience, from designing infrastructure to withstand extreme weather events to implementing sustainable practices that mitigate environmental impact and ensure long-term survival in an unpredictable world.
5. **Water Management and Sanitation:** Explore ways to locate, purify, and manage water while maintaining proper sanitation to prevent disease.
6. **Reestablishing Communication and Transportation:** Rebuild communication networks and restore transportation systems to reconnect communities and support recovery.
7. **Power and Energy Solutions:** Tap into renewable energy sources like solar and wind, and learn how to store and conserve energy effectively.
8. **Rebuilding Governance and Social Structures:** Develop leadership, craft fair laws, and foster a resilient, cooperative community culture.
9. **Health and Medicine in a New World:** Establish community health systems, embrace traditional and herbal medicine, and prioritize preventive care.
10. **Education and Knowledge Preservation:** Build education systems and safeguard the knowledge that will shape future generations.
11. **Reconnecting with Nature:** Revive ecosystems, embrace sustainable agriculture, and prepare for environmental challenges ahead.

Each chapter is packed with actionable strategies and practical advice, ensuring you're ready not only to survive but to thrive—and to lay the foundation for a sustainable, resilient future.

The Journey Ahead

As you embark on this journey, it's vital to prepare yourself mentally and emotionally for the challenges that lie ahead. Rebuilding civilization is no small task. It demands not just physical readiness but also mental strength and a clear sense of purpose.

This book will urge you to think critically, plan effectively, and act with determination. It will inspire you to take ownership of your survival and the survival of your community. It will drive you to acquire new skills, think creatively, and adapt to evolving situations.

Above all, this book is about hope. It embodies the belief that, no matter how dire the circumstances, we can rebuild and create a better, more sustainable world. It highlights the power of community, collaboration toward shared goals, and the resilience of the human spirit.

The path ahead may be tough, but it is a journey worth taking. By the end, you will gain the knowledge, skills, and confidence to tackle any challenge. You will be equipped to not only survive but lead in rebuilding a flourishing, sustainable civilization.

So, take a deep breath, gather your resolve, and let's embark on this journey together. The future rests in your hands.

Chapter 1: Surviving the Collapse

Amid societal collapse, survival becomes your top priority. This chapter outlines the critical actions needed to meet your basic needs, safeguard yourself and your loved ones, and take the first steps toward rebuilding in a drastically changed world.

1.1 Understanding the Collapse

Societal collapse often evokes images of sudden, devastating events—natural disasters, wars, or economic crises that disrupt entire communities and nations. Yet, the reality of collapse is typically far more intricate and multifaceted. Grasping the potential causes, identifying the warning signs of an approaching collapse, and preparing for its psychological effects on individuals and communities are critical initial steps to securing your survival and that of those around you.

Common Causes of Societal Collapse

Throughout history, civilizations have risen and fallen, often due to an interplay of factors that overwhelm the systems sustaining societies. These causes can be grouped into environmental, economic, political, and social categories, often intersecting and amplifying one another.

Environmental Causes: Environmental degradation frequently precedes societal collapse. Overpopulation, deforestation, soil erosion, and water scarcity are examples of how human activity undermines the natural systems that sustain life. Climate change, with its capacity to disrupt weather patterns, raise sea levels, and intensify extreme weather events, poses a contemporary threat to global stability.

Historical examples include the Mayans and Easter Islanders, whose societies faltered due to environmental mismanagement. For the Mayans, deforestation and soil exhaustion led to agricultural decline, famine, and unrest. The Easter Islanders overexploited their resources, resulting in deforestation, loss of wildlife, and societal breakdown.

Economic Causes: Economic collapse stems from factors like hyperinflation, financial crises, or resource depletion. Failed economies often erode the stability on which societies rely. The Roman Empire's decline, for instance, involved economic mismanagement, inflation, and overdependence on slave labor, destabilizing its economy and contributing to its fall.

In modern history, the Great Depression highlights how economic failure can trigger widespread suffering and upheaval. Though recovery followed, the Depression left lasting scars and spurred changes in economic governance, underscoring the link between economic and societal resilience.

Political Causes: Political instability and corruption can destabilize civilizations. Governments that fail to maintain order, deliver services, or meet public needs risk societal disintegration. The Soviet Union exemplifies how political corruption, coupled with economic decline, led to the collapse of a superpower. Its inability to address mounting challenges caused the state to fragment, bringing widespread hardship and a reordering of regional power.

Social Causes: Social decay, characterized by rising inequality, loss of cohesion, and moral decline, also undermines societies. When social trust deteriorates, conflicts arise, and communities fracture. The French Revolution demonstrates how inequality and disconnection between rulers and the populace sparked a violent uprising, reshaping French society.

Signs of Impending Collapse

Identifying the warning signs of an impending collapse is essential for effective preparation and response. These signs often emerge as a convergence of the factors mentioned earlier, creating a perfect storm capable of overwhelming even resilient societies.

One early indicator is the deterioration of infrastructure and public services. When roads, bridges, and utilities fall into disrepair, and essential services like healthcare, education, and law enforcement degrade, it signals that the systems supporting society are faltering.

Another critical sign is the erosion of trust in institutions. When governments, financial systems, and social structures are perceived as corrupt or ineffective, public confidence wanes, increasing the likelihood of social unrest and violence.

Economic instability, such as rising unemployment, inflation, and shortages of vital goods, is another red flag. As people struggle to meet basic needs, crime may rise, and social order can unravel, creating a cycle of escalating instability.

Environmental degradation, though slower to unfold, also serves as a warning. Persistent droughts, falling agricultural yields, and resource depletion are clear indicators that a society could be approaching a tipping point.

The Psychological Impact of Collapse on Individuals and Communities

The psychological toll of societal collapse cannot be underestimated. The loss of stability, security, and normalcy often triggers widespread fear, anxiety, and trauma. Individuals may experience emotions ranging from denial and anger to despair and hopelessness, while communities can fracture as survival becomes the focus, trust erodes, and social cohesion unravels.

In the early stages, denial is a common reaction. Many people hold onto the hope that normalcy will return, even as evidence of collapse mounts. This denial can delay necessary preparations, leaving individuals and communities vulnerable when the crisis fully unfolds.

As reality sets in, fear and anxiety often dominate. Uncertainty about the future, coupled with a loss of control over circumstances, heightens stress and can lead to panic. These emotional reactions can worsen the collapse, as decisions driven by fear often undermine reason and stability.

Over time, the trauma of enduring collapse can have long-lasting effects on mental health. Conditions like depression, post-traumatic stress disorder (PTSD), and other psychological issues may become widespread, particularly after prolonged or violent crises. Communities may find it challenging to rebuild trust and cohesion, as the collective trauma deepens divisions and fuels conflict.

Recognizing the psychological impact of societal collapse is crucial for preparing yourself and your community. Strengthening mental resilience, nurturing strong social connections, and crafting a clear plan of action can mitigate these effects, improving your chances of surviving and thriving in a post-collapse world.

1.2 Immediate Survival Needs

When the fabric of society begins to fray and collapse is imminent or already in progress, the most immediate concern becomes survival. In such a scenario, all the luxuries and conveniences of modern life fade into insignificance compared to the primal needs of water, food, and shelter. Securing these basic necessities is the first and most crucial step to ensure that you and your loved ones can withstand the initial shock of a collapsing civilization.

Securing Water Sources

Water is the most essential resource for survival, as the human body can only last a few days without it. In a post-collapse world, the infrastructure delivering clean water may no longer function. Your top priority, therefore, is to secure a consistent and safe water source.

In the immediate aftermath, there are several ways to find and purify water. Natural sources like rivers, lakes, or springs can provide a lifeline, but contamination risks increase in a collapsed society without effective waste management. Thus, all water must be treated before consumption.

Boiling water is a simple and highly effective method of purification, eliminating most pathogens. If fuel is available, bring the water to a rolling boil for at least one minute; at higher altitudes, boil for three minutes.

When boiling is impractical, chemical treatments are a viable alternative. Water purification tablets, often containing iodine or chlorine, offer a short-term solution. Follow the instructions carefully, as improper use may leave water unsafe. Portable filters, such as those with activated carbon or ceramic elements, can also remove many contaminants, though they may not eliminate all viruses. Redundancy in purification methods is essential to ensure a reliable water supply.

Rainwater harvesting is another effective strategy, particularly in areas with frequent rainfall. Simple systems can collect rainwater from roofs or surfaces into storage containers. However, rainwater should be treated before drinking, especially if it's collected from potentially contaminated surfaces.

In extreme cases where natural sources are scarce, methods like dew collection or solar stills may be necessary. Dew collection involves using absorbent materials to gather moisture from plants or surfaces in the early morning, while solar stills use sunlight to evaporate and condense water from soil or vegetation. These methods can be labor-intensive and produce small quantities but can be lifesaving in arid conditions.

Long-term water storage is equally critical. Large, food-grade containers can hold reserves for times when fresh water is unavailable. Store water in a cool, dark place and check regularly for contamination. Adding a small amount of chlorine bleach (free of additives) can help prevent bacteria and algae growth, extending shelf life.

Establishing a dependable water supply involves not only addressing immediate needs but also creating sustainable systems for the future. Conserve water diligently, monitor for contamination, and always seek out and test new sources. Water is life, and in a collapsed society, it may become your most valuable asset.

Finding or Constructing Shelter

Shelter is the second most vital component of survival. Without functioning infrastructure and services, protecting yourself from the elements and securing a safe place to rest becomes critical. The type of shelter you need will depend on your environment, available resources, and the specific challenges posed by societal collapse.

If you can remain in your home, your first priority is to assess and fortify it against both natural and human threats. Secure all entry points—doors, windows, and other vulnerabilities—by reinforcing weak areas with materials like plywood, metal bars, or improvised barricades. A well-defended home not only shields you from the elements but also deters looters and other dangers.

If staying home isn't feasible due to safety concerns, environmental hazards, or other factors, finding or building alternative shelter becomes essential. Location is paramount when selecting a site—natural protection from hillsides, dense forests, or caves offers shelter from the elements while providing camouflage and added security against threats.

In the absence of natural shelters, you may need to construct your own. In wooded areas, a lean-to made from branches and leaves is quick to assemble and offers basic wind and rain protection. A debris hut, insulated with leaves, grass, or other materials, can retain body heat in colder climates and provides more substantial protection.

In open areas with limited natural materials, creativity is key. Tarps, ponchos, or plastic sheeting can serve as temporary shelters. Vehicles can also be used as makeshift shelters, though ensuring proper ventilation is crucial to avoid carbon monoxide poisoning if the engine is used for warmth.

Urban environments offer the possibility of shelter in abandoned buildings, but they come with risks. Inspect any building thoroughly for structural stability, hidden occupants, or hazards like gas leaks or contamination. Once inside, secure the building and designate a safe area for sleeping, storing supplies, and planning.

For long-term survival, consider how to transition a temporary shelter into a more permanent home. Reinforce walls, expand living spaces, or dig a root cellar for food storage. These improvements enhance comfort, durability, and the shelter's ability to accommodate more people or supplies over time.

Psychologically, having a secure and organized space is invaluable in uncertain times. Even basic shelters can provide stability and mental health benefits. Personalizing your space—organizing gear, creating a comfortable sleeping area, or setting up a small "living room"—can foster a sense of normalcy and well-being.

Finally, always have a contingency plan. No shelter is completely secure, and unforeseen circumstances may force you to relocate. Identify fallback options in your area, and if possible, prepare them with basic supplies and equipment. Knowing you have a backup shelter increases your resilience and peace of mind in the event your primary shelter is compromised.

Emergency Food Supplies and Nutrition

The third cornerstone of immediate survival is food. While the human body can endure weeks without it, a lack of proper nutrition quickly leads to weakness, impaired thinking, and vulnerability to illness—none of which are acceptable in a post-collapse environment.

In the first days and weeks after a collapse, focus on consuming perishable foods. Refrigerated and frozen items will spoil quickly without power, so prioritize these in your meals. Cook and eat them while still safe, and explore preservation methods like drying, salting, or smoking meats to extend their usability without refrigeration.

When perishable supplies run out, shift to non-perishable foods. Ideally, you'll have stockpiled calorie-dense, nutritionally balanced options like canned goods, dried beans, rice, pasta, and grains. These foods are long-lasting and require minimal preparation. Regularly rotate your stock to maintain freshness and avoid spoilage.

Water is equally critical for food preparation, especially when relying on dried goods. Ensure your water supply covers not just drinking needs but also cooking. Learn simple recipes requiring few ingredients and minimal water. Basic cooking techniques like boiling, steaming, and baking over improvised ovens or open flames will become essential.

Nutrition is another key concern. While calorie intake is vital, a balanced diet is crucial for long-term health. Fresh fruits and vegetables will become scarce, so plan accordingly. Canned vegetables, dried fruits, and multivitamins can help fill the gap, though they are not substitutes for fresh produce.

This underscores the importance of foraging, hunting, and gardening. Even with a stocked pantry, these skills grow increasingly valuable over time. Foraging for wild edibles can supplement your diet with vital nutrients. Learn to identify safe local plants, such as dandelions, clover, and wild berries, while avoiding toxic species.

Hunting and fishing provide vital protein sources in a resource-scarce world. If you're unfamiliar with basic hunting techniques, now is the time to learn. Small game like rabbits, squirrels, and birds can be hunted with minimal gear, and fishing requires only a rod, line, and bait. Be mindful of sustainability to avoid depleting these resources.

Gardening offers the most sustainable solution for long-term food security. Even small gardens can yield significant amounts if you choose high-yield crops like potatoes, carrots, beans, and leafy greens. Composting can enrich your soil, and companion planting can maximize productivity.

If outdoor gardening isn't an option, sprouting seeds and legumes indoors provides a fresh, nutrient-rich food source with minimal space and effort. Sprouts are easy to grow and ready in days, making them an excellent addition to your survival plan.

In summary, securing water, shelter, and food requires preparation, adaptability, and the right strategies. Your approach will depend on your environment, resources, and challenges. By prioritizing these essentials and honing the skills to secure them, you enhance your ability to survive the initial stages of collapse and build a foundation for sustainable living.

1.3 Self-Defense and Security

As the initial shock of societal collapse subsides, a stark new reality sets in—one where ensuring the safety of yourself and your loved ones becomes critical. With the absence of organized law enforcement and social order, self-defense and security shift from theoretical ideas to essential daily survival practices. This section explores the strategies, tactics, and mindset required to safeguard yourself, your family, and your resources against various potential threats.

Basic Self-Defense Strategies

Self-defense begins with recognizing that you are your first and most dependable line of protection. In the power vacuum left by societal collapse, where the rule of law gives way to the rule of force, understanding basic self-defense principles becomes vital.

The foundation of self-defense is cultivating a mindset of vigilance. This involves staying constantly aware of your surroundings, identifying potential threats, and recognizing the baseline behavior of those nearby. In a post-collapse world, situational awareness is your most valuable tool, enabling you to avoid many dangers before they escalate.

Physical self-defense training is equally important. While mastering martial arts may not be feasible, learning basic techniques can be life-saving. Focus on simple, effective moves that target an attacker's vulnerable areas, such as the eyes, throat, and groin. The goal is not prolonged engagement but disabling the attacker long enough to escape or neutralize the threat.

In some cases, weapons may be necessary for defense. Firearms are among the most effective tools, but they require proper training and maintenance. If you own a firearm, ensure you are proficient in its use, understand its limitations, and practice under varied conditions. Store firearms securely but within easy reach, as seconds can be critical in emergencies.

For those without access to firearms, improvised weapons can serve as alternatives. Knives, clubs, or even everyday objects like hammers or heavy flashlights can be effective. The key is mental readiness—be prepared to use these tools if needed and practice deploying them in potential scenarios.

Securing Your Perimeter

Securing your home or shelter from potential intruders is a vital element of post-collapse survival. With traditional security systems likely nonfunctional, you must rely on physical barriers, vigilance, and community cooperation to safeguard your perimeter.

Start by assessing your home or shelter for vulnerabilities. Identify all entry points, such as doors, windows, basements, and attics. Reinforce these with available materials—boards, metal bars, or even furniture can block access. Set up makeshift alarms, like cans on a string or bells on doors, to provide early warnings of attempted breaches.

Beyond reinforcing entry points, establish a layered defense around your perimeter. This might include fencing, barricades, or obstacles to hinder intruders and make it harder for them to approach unnoticed. Maintain a clear line of sight to these defenses from your shelter to monitor activity and respond promptly if necessary.

A key deterrent is the appearance of occupancy and preparedness. Homes that look occupied and secure are less likely to be targeted than those appearing abandoned or vulnerable. Use solar-powered or battery-operated lights to keep the area illuminated at night and maintain a visible presence during the day. Coordinating with neighbors to organize patrols or shared watch shifts can further bolster security for everyone.

Dealing with Potential Threats (Both Human and Environmental)

The threats you face in a post-collapse world are diverse and often unpredictable. Human threats, such as looters, desperate individuals, and organized groups, pose significant risks, while environmental dangers like wild animals, fires, and natural disasters can be equally perilous.

For human threats, deterrence is often your first line of defense. A well-secured home, visible security measures, and a reputation for readiness can dissuade many intruders. However, deterrence may not always suffice, and you must be prepared to act decisively if your defenses are breached.

When confronting an intruder, apply the principles of self-defense. Your response should be swift, decisive, and proportional to the threat. The goal is to protect yourself and your loved ones, not to seek unnecessary conflict. If possible, issue a clear warning before using force, as this can sometimes de-escalate a situation. However, be ready to act if the warning is ignored.

Organized groups or gangs present a more complex challenge, as their coordination and intent make them particularly dangerous. If such groups are active in your area, consider forming alliances with neighbors or community members. A coordinated defense is often far more effective than isolated individuals acting alone.

Environmental threats also demand preparation. Wild animals may become more aggressive or desperate in the absence of human activity, especially in areas where food is scarce. Learn about the wildlife in your region, their behaviors, and habitats. Secure your food supplies to avoid attracting animals, and remain vigilant about nesting or denning areas near your shelter.

Fire is another major hazard in a post-collapse environment. Without access to firefighting services, even small fires can escalate rapidly. Keep fire extinguishers readily available and ensure you know how to use them. Remove flammable materials near your shelter, and consider creating a firebreak if wildfires are a concern in your area.

Natural disasters such as storms, floods, and earthquakes may also pose heightened risks without organized emergency services. Understand the specific hazards in your region and take proactive steps to mitigate them. This may involve reinforcing your shelter, developing an evacuation plan, or stockpiling supplies in a safe and accessible location.

In summary, self-defense and security are essential for surviving in a post-collapse world. By identifying potential threats and taking proactive measures to safeguard yourself and your community, you can improve your chances of navigating both the immediate aftermath and the uncertain times ahead. Preparedness, vigilance, and decisive action remain your strongest defenses in the absence of the rule of law.

1.4 Forming a Survival Group

In the chaotic uncertainty of a post-collapse world, attempting to "go it alone" is not only risky but often unsustainable. The complexities of survival in such an environment are better addressed through cooperation and collective effort. Building a survival group—a community that combines skills, resources, and strengths—can significantly improve your chances of surviving and even thriving in the aftermath. This section examines the critical role of community in survival, strategies for identifying and recruiting members, and the roles and responsibilities within the group.

The Importance of Community in Survival

Human beings are inherently social, and throughout history, communities have been essential for survival and progress. In a societal collapse, the importance of community becomes even greater. The sheer number of tasks required for survival—securing resources, defending against threats, managing healthcare, and maintaining morale—can quickly overwhelm an individual or small family. A well-organized survival group distributes these tasks, enabling a more efficient and sustainable approach to survival.

One major advantage of forming a survival group is the variety of skills and knowledge its members contribute. In a group, individuals can specialize—one person may have medical expertise, another might excel in hunting and fishing, while someone else focuses on construction and repairs. This specialization allows the group to function more effectively, with members leveraging their strengths for the collective good.

A survival group also provides vital mental and emotional support. The psychological strain of living in a post-collapse world—marked by stress, fear, and grief—can weigh heavily on individuals. Being part of a group offers emotional support, shared responsibility, and a sense of belonging, helping to counteract feelings of isolation and despair.

Community is equally crucial for defense. A well-coordinated group is far better equipped to handle threats, whether human or environmental, than an individual alone. Members can share watch duties, implement defense strategies, and respond more effectively to emergencies. A group's presence can also deter potential aggressors, who are less likely to target a well-organized community than a solitary person.

In long-term survival scenarios, groups are also better suited to undertaking large-scale projects that would be unmanageable for an individual. These include building and maintaining infrastructure, growing food, and establishing trade with other groups. Such activities not only improve survival odds but also lay the foundation for rebuilding a functioning society.

Identifying and Recruiting Members

The process of forming a survival group begins with identifying potential members. Ideally, you should start this process well before a collapse occurs, as building trust and establishing roles takes time. When selecting members for your group, consider both the practical skills they bring and their personal qualities. Look for individuals who are resourceful, adaptable, and capable of working well under stress. Character is just as important as skill—someone who is reliable, trustworthy, and cooperative will be far more valuable than a highly skilled individual who cannot work well with others.

Consider people within your existing social network—friends, family, neighbors, and colleagues—as potential group members. These individuals are often the best candidates because you already have a relationship with them, which can make it easier to establish trust and cooperation. However, be mindful of the dynamics within these relationships; not all friends or family members will be suited for the rigors of survival in a post-collapse world.

When approaching potential members, be clear about your intentions and the goals of the group. Discuss the benefits of forming a group and the responsibilities that come with it. It's important that everyone understands the commitment required and is willing to contribute. Honesty and transparency are key—everyone should be on the same page regarding the group's objectives, values, and expectations.

Skills are an essential consideration, but so is diversity. A well-rounded group should have a mix of abilities, including medical knowledge, tactical skills, practical trades (such as carpentry, plumbing, and mechanics), and agricultural experience. In addition to these practical skills, consider the importance of leadership and decision-making abilities. Every group needs individuals who can take charge in a crisis, make informed decisions, and mediate conflicts.

Once you have identified potential members, the next step is to hold discussions and possibly even group meetings to gauge how well everyone works together. This is an opportunity to assess interpersonal dynamics and resolve any potential issues before they arise in a survival scenario. It's also a time to start building trust—members should feel comfortable relying on each other and sharing responsibilities.

Roles and Responsibilities Within the Group

Once your group is formed, establishing clear roles and responsibilities is crucial for ensuring that everyone contributes effectively and that the group operates smoothly. While flexibility is important—members may need to adapt to changing circumstances—having defined roles can prevent confusion and ensure that all necessary tasks are covered.

Start by identifying the essential functions that the group needs to perform regularly. These might include security, food production, medical care, communication, and resource management. Assign roles based on each member's strengths and expertise. For example, someone with a background in medicine could take on the role of the group's primary medic, while someone with tactical training might be responsible for security.

In addition to primary roles, consider secondary roles or cross-training members in multiple areas. This ensures that the group remains functional even if a key member is incapacitated or unavailable. For instance, if the group's primary food producer falls ill, someone else should be able to step in and manage food-related tasks.

Leadership is another critical aspect of group dynamics. Decide early on how leadership will be structured. Will the group have a single leader, or will it operate under a council or committee system? How will decisions be made—by consensus, majority vote, or by a designated leader? Clarifying these structures and processes from the outset can prevent disputes and ensure that the group operates efficiently.

Regular communication is essential for maintaining group cohesion and addressing any issues that arise. Establish regular meetings or check-ins where members can discuss challenges, share updates, and plan for the future. This is also an opportunity to reinforce the group's goals and ensure that everyone remains aligned with the overall mission.

Finally, consider the importance of discipline and accountability within the group. In a survival situation, the stakes are high, and mistakes or negligence can have serious consequences. Establishing clear expectations and holding members accountable for their responsibilities is necessary for the group's overall well-being. However, this should be balanced with compassion and support—everyone will face challenges and difficulties, and a strong group is one that helps its members overcome these obstacles together.

In conclusion, forming a survival group is one of the most effective strategies for increasing your chances of surviving a societal collapse. By building a community that values cooperation, trust, and shared responsibility, you create a resilient and adaptable unit capable of facing the myriad challenges that a post-collapse world presents. Whether you are planning for short-term survival or long-term rebuilding, the strength and solidarity of your group will be your greatest asset.

Chapter 2: Establishing Resilient Food Systems for Long-Term Survival

Sustaining life demands a dependable food source. This chapter delves into creating a sustainable food supply through gardening, foraging, hunting, and preservation, ensuring long-term resilience and success for your community.

2.1 Adaptive Gardening for Survival

In the wake of a societal collapse, the ability to produce your own food becomes not just a convenience but a necessity. Gardening for survival goes beyond the leisurely pursuit of horticulture; it is a critical skill that can mean the difference between life and death. Establishing a sustainable food supply through gardening requires careful planning, resourcefulness, and a deep understanding of your environment. This chapter will explore the essential principles of survival gardening, including selecting crops that thrive in various climates, maximizing yields with limited resources, and maintaining soil health through crop rotation and effective soil management.

Selecting Crops That Thrive in Various Climates

A key aspect of survival gardening is selecting crops that thrive in your specific climate and conditions. Unlike modern agriculture, reliant on controlled environments and heavy inputs, survival gardening must adapt to natural limitations. This means growing hardy, resilient crops capable of yielding reliable harvests under challenging circumstances.

Begin by evaluating your local climate—temperature, rainfall, and the length of the growing season are critical factors. For cooler climates with short growing seasons, frost-tolerant crops like potatoes, kale, and carrots are ideal. In warmer regions with extended seasons, heat-loving crops like sweet potatoes, okra, and tomatoes excel.

Resilience to local challenges such as pests, diseases, and extreme weather is another vital consideration. Heirloom and indigenous plant varieties, naturally adapted to specific regions over generations, are often more robust than hybrid breeds. These traditional crops are better equipped to withstand environmental challenges, making them invaluable in a survival garden.

Nutritional value is equally important. A survival garden must supply not just calories but also essential vitamins and minerals to maintain health and energy. Leafy greens like spinach and chard are rich in vitamins A and C, while legumes such as beans and peas provide protein and amino acids. Root vegetables like carrots and beets offer beta-carotene and folate, supporting immune function and overall wellness.

Beyond staples, include a variety of herbs and medicinal plants. Herbs like basil, thyme, and oregano enhance flavor and possess antimicrobial properties to reduce illness risk. Medicinal plants, such as echinacea, calendula, and garlic, provide natural remedies for common ailments, offering an essential supplement when conventional medicine is unavailable.

By thoughtfully selecting crops and incorporating medicinal and nutritional diversity, your survival garden can become a reliable and sustainable resource, securing health and sustenance in a challenging world.

Maximizing Yield with Limited Resources

In a post-collapse world, resources such as water, fertilizer, and space may be scarce. Therefore, maximizing the yield of your garden with minimal inputs is essential. Techniques such as companion planting, vertical gardening, and mulching can significantly increase productivity while conserving resources.

Companion planting is a traditional method that involves growing complementary plants together to improve growth, reduce pests, and enhance soil fertility. For example, planting beans alongside corn and squash (the traditional "Three Sisters" method) allows the beans to fix nitrogen in the soil, benefiting the corn and squash, while the squash provides ground cover that helps retain moisture and suppress weeds.

Vertical gardening is another effective strategy, especially in areas with limited space. Growing plants on trellises, arbors, or stacked planters allows you to make the most of available space and can increase yields per square foot. This method is particularly useful for crops like beans, peas, and cucumbers, which naturally climb and can produce abundant harvests in a small footprint.

Mulching is a simple yet powerful technique for conserving water, suppressing weeds, and improving soil health. By covering the soil with organic materials such as straw, leaves, or grass clippings, you can reduce evaporation, keep the soil temperature stable, and add valuable nutrients back into the soil as the mulch decomposes.

In addition to these techniques, it's important to practice water conservation in your garden. Collecting rainwater, using drip irrigation systems, and watering during the early morning or late evening can reduce water usage while ensuring that your plants receive the moisture they need to thrive.

Crop Rotation and Soil Management

Maintaining soil fertility is crucial for the long-term productivity of your garden. Soil that is overused or improperly managed will quickly become depleted of nutrients, leading to reduced yields and increased vulnerability to pests and diseases. Crop rotation and effective soil management practices are key to sustaining a healthy, productive garden over the long term.

Crop rotation involves changing the types of crops grown in a specific area of your garden from season to season. This practice helps prevent the buildup of pests and diseases that are specific to certain plants and reduces the depletion of particular nutrients from the soil. For example, after growing nitrogen-hungry crops like corn or cabbage, it's beneficial to plant legumes such as beans or peas in the same area the following season. These plants fix nitrogen in the soil, replenishing this essential nutrient and preparing the soil for the next cycle of crops.

In addition to crop rotation, consider incorporating cover crops, also known as green manures, into your gardening practice. Cover crops such as clover, rye, or vetch can be planted during the off-season to protect the soil from erosion, improve its structure, and add organic matter when they are turned under. These crops help maintain soil health by enhancing microbial activity, increasing nutrient availability, and improving moisture retention.

Composting is another critical component of soil management. By recycling kitchen scraps, garden waste, and other organic materials into compost, you can create a rich, nutrient-dense soil amendment that enhances fertility and structure. Composting not only reduces waste but also improves the quality of your soil, promoting healthier plant growth and higher yields.

Finally, it's essential to monitor the pH and nutrient levels of your soil regularly. Soil testing kits are relatively inexpensive and can provide valuable information about the health of your soil. Based on the results, you can adjust your soil management practices, such as adding lime to raise the pH or incorporating specific nutrients to address deficiencies.

By carefully selecting crops, maximizing yields with limited resources, and maintaining soil health through rotation and management practices, you can establish a sustainable and productive food supply in your garden. This foundation of food security will not only support your survival in the immediate aftermath of a collapse but also contribute to the long-term resilience and self-sufficiency of your community.

2.2 Foraging and Hunting

In a post-collapse world, where conventional food supplies may be disrupted or depleted, the ability to forage and hunt can be a critical means of securing sustenance. Foraging and hunting not only provide essential calories and nutrients but also reconnect us with the natural environment, teaching us to live in harmony with the land. This section will delve into the fundamentals of identifying edible wild plants, mastering basic hunting and trapping techniques, and effectively preserving and storing wild foods for long-term use.

Identifying Edible Wild Plants

Foraging is an ancient skill that sustained humans for millennia before agriculture. The ability to identify and harvest wild edible plants is invaluable in survival scenarios, providing nutrition when cultivated crops are unavailable or insufficient. However, foraging demands extensive knowledge, as many plants are both edible and toxic, often difficult to distinguish.

Start by familiarizing yourself with the local flora. Use a reliable, region-specific field guide to identify edible plants, their habitats, and seasonal availability. Wild plants often surpass cultivated ones in nutritional value. For instance, dandelion greens are rich in vitamins A, C, and K, while nettles offer iron, calcium, and protein.

When encountering unknown plants, apply the "Universal Edibility Test," especially in survival situations. This involves testing each part—leaves, roots, stems, flowers—by touching it to your skin, lips, and tongue before consuming a small amount. While helpful, this method is not foolproof and should be a last resort when no other food is available.

Reliable wild edibles include acorns, which can be leached of tannins and made into flour, and cattails, with edible roots and shoots. Berries like blackberries, raspberries, and elderberries are rich in antioxidants. Wild greens such as lamb's quarters, chickweed, and purslane are nutritious and can be eaten raw or cooked. Mushrooms, while a valuable food source, require extreme caution, as many poisonous varieties resemble edible ones. Unless you have expert knowledge or a detailed guide, avoid wild mushrooms entirely.

Foraging also involves gathering nuts, seeds, and tubers, which provide essential fats and carbohydrates. Walnuts, hazelnuts, and chestnuts are excellent sources of protein and healthy fats, while tubers like wild potatoes and Jerusalem artichokes offer starch and satiety. These are often abundant in the fall when other resources may dwindle.

Sustainable foraging is essential to preserve wild food sources. Avoid overharvesting any plant, leaving enough for reproduction and for other foragers and wildlife. Be mindful of the environment to prevent long-term damage to ecosystems. By practicing sustainable foraging, you contribute to ecological health and ensure the availability of resources for future use.

Basic Hunting and Trapping Techniques

While foraging provides plant-based foods, hunting and trapping supply protein-rich meat essential for energy and muscle maintenance in survival situations. These activities require a distinct skill set, including knowledge of animal behavior, weapon or trap proficiency, and the ability to process and preserve meat.

Before hunting, familiarize yourself with the types of game in your area. Different animals have unique habitats, behaviors, and peak activity times, influencing your approach. For instance, deer are active at dawn and dusk, often near water, while rabbits feed along field edges or in brushy areas. Understanding these patterns improves your success.

Common hunting weapons include firearms, bows, and slingshots. Firearms are highly effective for large game like deer or wild boar but require ammunition, which may be scarce post-collapse. Bows, particularly compound bows, are quieter and less reliant on ammunition, suitable for both large and small game. Slingshots, while less powerful, are effective for small animals like birds or squirrels and are lightweight and portable.

Trapping is an essential technique, especially for small game, as it allows multiple captures simultaneously. Effective traps include snares, deadfalls, and pit traps. Snares, simple wire or cord loops, can be set in high-traffic areas. Deadfall traps use a weighted object to kill the animal instantly upon activation. Pit traps involve digging a camouflaged hole that traps animals when they step on the cover.

Careful trap placement is crucial. Look for signs of animal activity—tracks, droppings, or disturbed vegetation—and set traps in these areas. Regularly check traps to prevent unnecessary suffering and ensure fresh meat.

Processing game requires skill to ensure meat is safe to eat and properly preserved. Field dressing, or removing internal organs, should be done promptly to avoid spoilage. The meat can then be butchered into usable cuts. Large game may be quartered, while small animals like rabbits can be skinned and gutted in one step.

By mastering these techniques, you can reliably secure protein-rich food, a critical component of survival.

Preserving and Storing Wild Foods

Once you've harvested wild plants or game, preserving and storing these foods is crucial to ensure a stable food supply over time. Preservation techniques such as drying, smoking, salting, and pickling have been used for centuries and remain effective methods for extending the shelf life of food in the absence of refrigeration.

Drying is one of the simplest and most versatile methods of preservation, suitable for both plant-based foods and meat. For plant foods like fruits, vegetables, and herbs, drying can be accomplished by hanging them in a well-ventilated area out of direct sunlight, or by using a solar dehydrator. Meat can be dried to create jerky, a lightweight and portable food that can last for months when stored properly. Thinly slice the meat, season it with salt and spices, and then dry it over low heat or in the sun until it is completely dehydrated.

Smoking is another effective preservation method, particularly for meat and fish. The process involves exposing the food to smoke from burning wood, which not only dehydrates it but also imparts a smoky flavor and inhibits the growth of bacteria. Cold smoking, done at lower temperatures, is ideal for longer preservation, while hot smoking, at higher temperatures, cooks the food while also preserving it. Both methods require a smokehouse or smoker, which can be constructed from simple materials.

Salting is an ancient technique that relies on the antimicrobial properties of salt to preserve food. Salt draws moisture out of the food, creating an environment where bacteria cannot thrive. Meat can be salted by rubbing it with a generous amount of salt and storing it in a cool, dry place. The meat can then be soaked in water before cooking to remove some of the excess salt. Fish is often preserved by packing it in layers of salt and storing it in barrels or jars.

Pickling is another method that involves submerging food in a solution of vinegar, salt, and spices. The acidity of the vinegar creates a hostile environment for bacteria, allowing the food to be stored for extended periods. Vegetables such as cucumbers, peppers, and cabbage are commonly pickled, but fruits and even eggs can be preserved this way as well.

Root cellaring is a traditional method of storing root vegetables, such as potatoes, carrots, and onions, in a cool, dark, and humid environment. A root cellar can be as simple as a pit dug into the ground or a more elaborate underground room. The key is to maintain a consistent temperature and humidity level to prevent the food from spoiling. Root cellaring is particularly useful in regions with cold winters, where fresh produce would otherwise be difficult to obtain.

Finally, fermenting is a preservation technique that also enhances the nutritional value of food by promoting the growth of beneficial bacteria. Fermented foods such as sauerkraut, kimchi, and yogurt are not only preserved but also rich in probiotics, which support digestive health. Fermentation requires a controlled environment, usually at room temperature, and can take anywhere from a few days to several weeks, depending on the food and desired flavor.

By mastering these preservation techniques, you can create a stockpile of food that will sustain you through periods of scarcity, ensuring that you and your community have access to nutritious meals even in the most challenging conditions.

In conclusion, foraging and hunting are essential skills for establishing a sustainable food supply in a post-collapse world. By learning to identify and harvest wild plants, mastering basic hunting and trapping techniques, and preserving the food you gather, you can secure a reliable source of nutrition that complements your gardening efforts and enhances your overall resilience in the face of uncertainty.

2.3 Sustainable Animal Practices for a New Era

In a post-collapse world, animal husbandry becomes a vital component of a sustainable and reliable food supply. Raising and managing livestock provides consistent protein sources and additional resources like milk, eggs, wool, and manure for soil enrichment. Successfully establishing a livestock system requires selecting species suited to your environment, building appropriate shelters, and employing effective breeding and management practices. This section outlines key considerations for choosing the right animals, constructing and maintaining shelters, and managing herds to ensure long-term sustainability.

Choosing the Right Livestock for Sustainability

Choosing the right livestock is the cornerstone of successful animal husbandry in a survival scenario. Your selection should consider geographic location, available resources, climate, and the specific needs of your group. Opt for animals that are hardy, easy to manage, and capable of thriving on forage or minimal supplemental feed.

Chickens are versatile and low-maintenance, requiring little space while foraging much of their food. They provide a steady supply of protein-rich eggs and can be raised for meat. Their manure enriches garden soil, making them a valuable addition to a sustainable farm. Hardy breeds like Rhode Island Reds, Plymouth Rocks, and Leghorns are ideal for small-scale farming.

Goats are excellent in areas with limited land or sparse vegetation. Adaptable and resilient, they thrive where other livestock might struggle. Goats provide milk for direct consumption or processing into cheese, yogurt, and butter, as well as a reliable source of meat. Their manure is an excellent fertilizer, and their ability to graze on diverse plants, including brush, makes them helpful for managing overgrowth. Breeds like Nubian, Alpine, and Boer goats are suited for both milk and meat.

Sheep are valued for wool, which can be used for clothing and blankets, as well as milk and meat. They are well-suited to cooler climates, grazing on pasture to reduce the need for supplemental feed. Productive and hardy breeds such as Dorset, Merino, and Suffolk are ideal for survival farming.

Rabbits are a compact and efficient meat source, requiring minimal space and reproducing quickly. They thrive on forage, garden scraps, and hay. Rabbit manure is nutrient-rich and can be directly applied to gardens without composting. Popular meat breeds include New Zealand, Californian, and Flemish Giant.

Consider also raising ducks or geese for their unique advantages. Ducks are exceptional foragers in wet environments, providing eggs and meat while being less disease-prone than chickens. Geese are effective grazers and natural weed controllers, offering meat and feathers in addition to their ecological benefits.

When selecting livestock, consider immediate benefits and long-term sustainability. Factors like reproductive rates, feed efficiency, disease resistance, and pest tolerance are crucial. Additionally, assess each animal's contribution to the farm ecosystem, such as manure for compost or pest control through grazing or foraging.

Building and Maintaining Shelters for Animals

Once you have selected your livestock, the next step is to provide them with adequate shelter. Proper housing is essential for protecting animals from the elements, predators, and disease, as well as for ensuring their comfort and productivity.

The design and construction of animal shelters will vary depending on the species, climate, and available materials, but some general principles apply across all types of livestock.

Shelters should provide protection from extreme weather conditions, including heat, cold, wind, and rain. In colder climates, shelters should be insulated or constructed with materials that help retain heat, such as straw or wood. In warmer climates, good ventilation is critical to prevent overheating and ensure a constant flow of fresh air. Consider building shelters with adjustable features, such as windows or vents, that can be opened or closed depending on the weather.

Chickens require a secure coop to protect them from predators such as foxes, raccoons, and hawks. The coop should include nesting boxes for egg-laying, roosting bars for sleeping, and enough space for the birds to move around comfortably. A general rule of thumb is to provide at least 2-3 square feet per chicken inside the coop, with additional space in an outdoor run. The coop should be raised off the ground to prevent moisture buildup and deter burrowing predators. Regular cleaning and maintenance are essential to prevent the buildup of ammonia from droppings, which can lead to respiratory issues.

Goats need a shelter that protects them from the elements while allowing them to roam freely. A three-sided shed is often sufficient in milder climates, while a fully enclosed barn or shed may be necessary in colder or wetter regions. Goats are notorious for their curiosity and climbing abilities, so shelters should be sturdy and secure to prevent escapes. Additionally, goats require space to graze and forage, so ensure that their shelter opens onto a secure pasture or paddock.

Sheep require similar shelter to goats, with the addition of shearing facilities if you plan to harvest wool. Their shelter should provide protection from wind and rain, and bedding such as straw should be provided to keep them warm and dry. Sheep are susceptible to foot rot, especially in wet conditions, so it's important to keep their shelter and surrounding area well-drained and clean.

Rabbits can be housed in hutches or cages, which should be elevated off the ground to protect them from predators and dampness. Hutches should include a sheltered area for sleeping and an open area with wire mesh for ventilation. If possible, provide rabbits with access to a secure outdoor pen where they can graze and exercise. Regularly clean and disinfect their living space to prevent the spread of disease.

In addition to shelter, all animals require access to clean water and a consistent supply of food. Water should be provided in containers that are easy to clean and prevent contamination from dirt or droppings. In colder climates, consider using heated water bowls or troughs to prevent freezing. Feed should be stored in a dry, secure location to protect it from pests and spoilage.

Maintaining animal shelters involves regular cleaning, repairs, and inspections to ensure the health and well-being of your livestock. Remove soiled bedding and waste regularly to prevent the buildup of harmful bacteria and parasites. Inspect shelters for signs of damage, such as holes or leaks, and repair them promptly to prevent predators from gaining access or to protect animals from the elements.

Properly designed and maintained shelters are crucial for the productivity and health of your livestock. They provide a safe and comfortable environment that supports their growth, reproduction, and overall well-being, ensuring a reliable source of food and other resources for your survival efforts.

2.4 Food Preservation Techniques

In a post-collapse world, maintaining a steady food supply is vital, but equally critical is preserving the food you harvest, forage, or hunt. Techniques such as canning, pickling, dehydration, smoking, and root cellaring are essential for extending food shelf life, ensuring access to nutritious meals even when fresh food is unavailable. This section delves into these preservation methods, equipping you with the knowledge and tools to store food effectively and safely for long-term use.

Canning and Pickling

Canning is an effective way to preserve fruits, vegetables, meats, and complete meals for long-term storage. The process involves placing food in jars and heating them to eliminate harmful microorganisms, creating a vacuum seal that prevents contamination. There are two primary canning methods: water bath canning and pressure canning.

Water bath canning is ideal for high-acid foods like fruits, tomatoes, and pickles, as their acidity prevents bacterial growth. This method requires a large pot with a lid, a rack to keep jars elevated, and canning jars with lids and bands. To can, fill jars with prepared food, leave headspace, seal the lids, and boil the jars for a specified time to ensure safety.

Pressure canning is necessary for low-acid foods such as vegetables, meats, and soups, which require higher temperatures to prevent contamination. A pressure canner uses steam under pressure to achieve temperatures above boiling. The process involves sealing jars in the pressure canner and processing them at specific pressure levels and times. This ensures the destruction of bacteria, including botulism spores, making the food safe for long-term storage.

Pickling is another effective preservation method, relying on vinegar, salt, and spices to create an acidic environment that inhibits bacterial growth. It can be done through fermentation or vinegar brining. Fermentation pickling, like making sauerkraut or kimchi, involves allowing food to ferment naturally in a brine, producing lactic acid for preservation while enhancing nutritional value with probiotics. Vinegar pickling, on the other hand, submerges food in a hot vinegar solution and seals it in jars, offering a quicker method for creating tangy, long-lasting pickles.

Both canning and pickling require meticulous attention to detail and strict adherence to safety guidelines to prevent foodborne illnesses. Always use clean, sterilized jars and follow tested recipes to ensure the correct balance of acidity, sugar, and salt. Regular practice builds confidence and skill, helping ensure your preserved foods are safe and reliable for long-term use.

Dehydration and Smoking

Dehydration is a simple and effective way to preserve a wide variety of foods, including fruits, vegetables, meats, and herbs. By removing the moisture from food, you inhibit the growth of bacteria, yeast, and mold, which require water to thrive. Dehydrated foods are lightweight, easy to store, and retain most of their nutritional value, making them an ideal option for long-term food storage.

There are several methods of dehydration, including sun drying, oven drying, and using a food dehydrator. **Sun drying** is one of the oldest methods and is still effective in warm, dry climates.

Foods like fruits, herbs, and thinly sliced vegetables can be spread out on screens or trays and left to dry in the sun. To protect the food from insects and dust, cover it with cheesecloth or netting. Sun drying requires several days of consistent warm temperatures and low humidity.

Oven drying is a more controlled method and can be done in any climate. To oven dry food, set your oven to a low temperature, typically around 140°F (60°C), and place the food on trays in a single layer. Leave the oven door slightly ajar to allow moisture to escape. The drying process can take several hours, depending on the food and thickness of the slices.

A **food dehydrator** is the most efficient method of dehydration, providing consistent heat and airflow to dry food quickly and evenly. Dehydrators come with adjustable temperature settings and multiple trays, allowing you to dry large quantities of food at once. Fruits like apples, bananas, and berries, as well as vegetables like tomatoes, peppers, and mushrooms, are all excellent candidates for dehydration. Once dried, store the food in airtight containers in a cool, dark place to maximize shelf life.

Smoking is another traditional method of preserving food, particularly meats and fish. Smoking involves exposing food to smoke from burning wood, which not only dehydrates the food but also imparts a smoky flavor and acts as a natural preservative. There are two main types of smoking: cold smoking and hot smoking.

Cold smoking is done at lower temperatures (below 90°F or 32°C) and is primarily used to flavor the food while still requiring additional preservation methods, such as curing or drying. Cold-smoked foods include items like smoked cheese, nuts, and cured meats like ham or bacon. Cold smoking typically takes several days and requires a smoker that can maintain low temperatures.

Hot smoking, on the other hand, cooks the food while smoking it, making it ready to eat immediately or store for later use. Hot smoking is done at temperatures between 150°F and 225°F (65°C to 107°C) and is ideal for meats like fish, poultry, and sausages. The smoking process can take several hours, depending on the type and thickness of the food. Once smoked, the food can be eaten immediately, refrigerated, or further preserved by drying or vacuum sealing.

Root Cellaring and Other Traditional Methods

Root cellaring is a time-tested method of storing vegetables and fruits in a cool, dark, and humid environment. Root cellars take advantage of the earth's natural insulation to maintain a stable temperature, usually between 32°F and 40°F (0°C to 4°C), and high humidity levels, which are ideal for storing root vegetables, apples, cabbages, and other produce that can last for several months.

To set up a root cellar, choose a location that is below ground or partially buried, such as a basement, shed, or even a pit dug into the ground. The key to a successful root cellar is maintaining the right conditions: cool, dark, and moist. Ventilation is important to prevent the buildup of ethylene gas, which can cause produce to spoil. Additionally, consider installing shelves or bins to keep the produce off the ground and allow air circulation around each item.

For those without access to a root cellar, **other traditional methods** of food preservation can be just as effective.

Fermentation is a natural process that not only preserves food but also enhances its nutritional value. Foods like sauerkraut, kimchi, and yogurt are all products of fermentation, which involves the conversion of sugars into alcohol or acids by beneficial bacteria. Fermented foods are rich in probiotics, which support digestive health and can be stored for long periods without refrigeration.

Salting and curing are also traditional methods used to preserve meats, fish, and even vegetables. Salting involves packing food in salt, which draws out moisture and creates an environment that is inhospitable to bacteria. Curing is similar but often involves the addition of sugar, nitrates, or spices to enhance flavor and preservation. Both methods require careful control of temperature and humidity to prevent spoilage and ensure the food remains safe to eat.

Freezing is another effective preservation method, though it requires a reliable source of cold temperatures, such as a natural icehouse or a makeshift freezer in colder climates. Frozen foods can last for months or even years if properly stored, retaining much of their original flavor and nutritional value. However, in a post-collapse scenario, access to consistent freezing temperatures may be limited, so freezing should be used in conjunction with other preservation methods.

By mastering these food preservation techniques, you can build a reliable stockpile of food that will sustain you and your community through the most challenging times. Whether you are canning, dehydrating, smoking, or root cellaring, each method offers a way to extend the life of your food, reduce waste, and ensure that you have access to nutritious, home-grown meals even when fresh supplies are scarce.

Chapter 3: Building and Maintaining Shelter

Shelter is essential for security and well-being. This chapter guides you in constructing and maintaining safe, durable structures to shield against the elements and serve as a sanctuary for your community.

3.1 Choosing Locations for Resilient Living

After a societal collapse, securing a safe, reliable shelter is a top priority. Shelter is more than a place to rest—it's your defense against the elements, a refuge from threats, and a cornerstone of survival. Building and maintaining a shelter starts with selecting an ideal location—one offering physical protection and access to essential resources like water, food, and building materials. This chapter outlines strategic approaches to choosing safe locations, evaluating natural resources and risks, and zoning your community for optimal functionality.

Strategic Considerations for Choosing a Safe Location

When selecting a location for your shelter, the first and most important consideration is safety. In a post-collapse environment, the risks you face can be numerous and unpredictable, including environmental hazards, human threats, and even wildlife. Your shelter's location should minimize these risks while maximizing your access to the resources needed for survival.

One of the primary considerations is **geographic elevation**. Choosing a location on higher ground offers several advantages. Elevated areas are less likely to flood, which is crucial if your region experiences heavy rainfall, snowmelt, or is near bodies of water. Additionally, higher ground can provide a strategic advantage in terms of visibility, allowing you to monitor your surroundings for potential threats and giving you more time to react. However, it's important to balance the benefits of elevation with accessibility—extremely high or difficult-to-reach areas may hinder your ability to gather resources or evacuate if necessary.

Another key factor is **proximity to water**. A reliable source of fresh water is essential for drinking, cooking, and sanitation. Ideally, your shelter should be within a short distance of a river, stream, or lake, but far enough away to avoid the dangers of flooding or waterborne diseases. If natural water sources are scarce, consider the feasibility of digging a well or setting up a rainwater harvesting system. Remember that water security is crucial for your long-term survival, so this should be one of the top priorities when selecting a location.

Access to food sources is also critical. If you plan to rely on foraging, hunting, or fishing, your shelter should be situated in an area with abundant wildlife, edible plants, and fishable waters. Forested areas often provide ample opportunities for hunting and gathering, while proximity to open fields or meadows can be beneficial for gardening and animal husbandry. Consider the sustainability of these resources as well—overexploitation can lead to scarcity, so choose a location where you can manage and renew these resources effectively.

Environmental hazards must be carefully assessed when choosing a location. Avoid areas that are prone to natural disasters such as earthquakes, landslides, or hurricanes. In regions where such events are common, look for areas with natural protection, such as hills or rock formations, that can shield you from wind, debris, or shifting earth. It's also wise to stay clear of industrial areas, which may become toxic in the event of a collapse, as well as regions with a history of environmental degradation.

The **climate** of the area should also influence your decision. Consider how the local weather patterns will affect your shelter and overall survival. In colder climates, you'll need to think about insulation and heating to survive harsh winters, while in warmer regions, ventilation and shade will be critical to avoid heatstroke and dehydration. If possible, select a location that offers some natural protection from extreme weather, such as a site with tree cover for shade or a south-facing slope for warmth.

Security is another paramount consideration. In a world where law and order may no longer exist, your shelter should be defensible against human threats. This means choosing a location that is not easily accessible or visible to outsiders. A remote location, or one that is naturally camouflaged by the landscape, can reduce the likelihood of being discovered by potential aggressors. Additionally, consider how you will secure the perimeter of your shelter—natural barriers like rivers or cliffs can provide added protection, but you may also need to construct fences or other fortifications to safeguard your home.

Finally, consider the **potential for expansion** and community development. While your immediate focus may be on creating a secure shelter for yourself and your family, it's important to think about the future. If conditions improve or you plan to establish a larger, self-sustaining community, you'll need space to expand your living area, grow food, and accommodate additional people. Choose a location that offers room for growth, whether that means building more structures, planting larger gardens, or raising more livestock.

In conclusion, selecting the right location for your shelter is a complex but crucial task that requires careful consideration of safety, resources, and long-term viability. By prioritizing these factors, you can establish a secure and sustainable base that will serve as the foundation for your survival and the potential rebuilding of your community. The right location not only provides immediate protection and resources but also sets the stage for resilience and growth in the face of an uncertain future.

3.2 Basic Construction Techniques

After selecting an ideal location for your shelter, the next crucial step is construction. Building a sturdy, weather-resistant structure with limited resources is a vital survival skill. Your shelter must shield you from the elements, provide security against threats, and offer comfort to support physical and mental health. This section covers essential construction techniques, including using available materials, crafting durable and weather-resistant structures, and ensuring proper insulation and ventilation for a safe, comfortable living environment.

Building with Available Materials

In a post-collapse world, modern building materials may be scarce, requiring reliance on natural or scavenged resources. Understanding the properties of these materials and their effective use is key to successful shelter construction.

Wood is one of the most accessible materials, especially in forested areas. Timber can be harvested using tools like axes and saws, then used as raw logs for cabins or split into planks for refined structures. Wooden shelters, such as lean-tos or log cabins, are relatively easy to build and provide good insulation, though fire safety must be prioritized due to wood's flammability.

Stone is a durable, fireproof material offering excellent protection against the elements. Readily available in some regions, it can be used for foundations, walls, or entire structures. Dry-stone walling involves stacking stones without mortar for sturdy barriers, while mortar-bound stone walls, using a sand, lime, and water mix, create long-lasting buildings. Though labor-intensive, stone offers superior durability and weather resistance.

Earth is another abundant material in many areas, with techniques like cob, adobe, and rammed earth providing versatile options. Cob, made from clay, sand, straw, and water, forms thick walls with excellent thermal properties. Adobe bricks, sun-dried and stacked, are strong and insulating, while rammed earth involves compacting soil into dense, solid walls. Each method suits different climates and resource availability.

Salvaged materials from abandoned structures can also be invaluable. Items like metal sheets, bricks, concrete blocks, windows, and doors can be repurposed for construction. Metal sheets work well for roofing or walls, while bricks and blocks provide strong foundations or structural walls. Scavenging requires creativity and caution to adapt materials safely and avoid hazards from unstable buildings.

Waterproofing is essential to protect your shelter from damage and discomfort caused by water infiltration. Thatch, made from grass or reeds, is an ancient and effective method if built correctly. Alternatively, tarps, plastic sheeting, or salvaged roofing materials can create a waterproof barrier. Ensuring a proper roof slope for runoff and tightly sealing seams is crucial for effective waterproofing.

A strong foundation is critical for shelter stability and durability. In wet or unstable soil, consider building on stilts or piers to prevent water damage and allow air circulation. On stable, dry ground, use stone or concrete blocks as a base, ensuring the soil is compacted and level before construction to maintain structural integrity over time.

Building a shelter with available materials requires ingenuity, adaptability, and knowledge of their properties. Whether using wood, stone, earth, or salvaged items, the key is selecting techniques suited to your resources and environment. By mastering these skills, you can create a shelter that is functional, protective, and a place of comfort in a post-collapse world.

Creating Sturdy, Weather-Resistant Structures

Once you have selected your materials and begun construction, the next step is to ensure that your shelter is sturdy and weather-resistant. A well-built shelter must be able to withstand the forces of nature, including wind, rain, snow, and extreme temperatures. This requires careful attention to the construction process, from the foundation to the roof, to ensure that your shelter is both durable and secure.

The **framework** of your shelter is its skeleton and provides the necessary support for the walls and roof. In most cases, the framework will be constructed from wood or metal, which offers the strength and flexibility needed to resist the stresses of wind and weight. **Timber framing**, a traditional method that uses large wooden beams and joints to create a strong structure, is ideal for building durable shelters. The beams are connected using mortise and tenon joints, which are both strong and flexible, allowing the structure to move slightly without breaking under pressure. **Metal framing** is another option, particularly if you have access to salvaged steel or aluminum. Metal frames are fireproof, resistant to pests, and can support heavier loads than wood.

After the framework is in place, the next step is to construct the **walls**. The choice of wall material will depend on the available resources and the specific needs of your environment. **Thick walls**, made from materials such as logs, stone, or earth, provide excellent insulation and protection from the elements. They also add structural strength, helping to anchor the shelter against wind and other forces. For example, **log walls** can be stacked horizontally, with each log interlocking at the corners, creating a sturdy and weather-tight structure. **Stone walls** can be built using either dry-stone techniques or with mortar to bind the stones together, depending on the level of permanence you desire.

Insulation is a crucial component of any shelter, particularly in regions with extreme temperatures. Proper insulation keeps your shelter warm in the winter and cool in the summer, reducing the need for additional heating or cooling resources. Natural materials such as **straw**, **wool**, **cotton**, and **sheep's wool** make excellent insulators and are often readily available. These materials can be packed into walls, floors, and ceilings to create a barrier that slows the transfer of heat. Additionally, **earth** can be used as an insulator by building thick walls or burying part of the structure underground to take advantage of the earth's natural thermal mass.

The **roof** is perhaps the most critical element in creating a weather-resistant shelter. A well-constructed roof protects the interior from rain, snow, and wind, while also providing insulation. **Pitched roofs** with a steep angle are ideal for shedding water and snow, preventing buildup that can lead to leaks or structural collapse. The roofing material should be chosen based on its ability to withstand the local climate—**metal roofing**, **thatch**, **shingles**, or **tile** are all viable options, depending on what is available. Ensure that the roof is properly sealed at all joints and edges to prevent water infiltration.

Ventilation is another key factor in maintaining a comfortable and healthy living environment. A well-ventilated shelter allows for the circulation of fresh air, reducing moisture buildup and the risk of mold and mildew. **Windows**, **vents**, and **chimneys** should be strategically placed to allow air to flow through the shelter without compromising insulation or security. In colder climates, it's important to design the ventilation system so that it can be adjusted to reduce heat loss in winter while allowing for airflow in the warmer months.

To further enhance the weather resistance of your shelter, consider **applying protective coatings** to the exterior. Natural oils, such as **linseed oil** or **beeswax**, can be used to seal wood and stone, providing a water-resistant barrier that also protects against pests and rot. In addition, **paint** or **lime wash** can be applied to exterior walls to create a durable, weather-resistant surface that reflects heat and protects against moisture.

In conclusion, creating a sturdy, weather-resistant structure is essential for long-term survival in a post-collapse world. By carefully selecting materials, constructing a strong framework, and incorporating proper insulation and ventilation, you can build a shelter that will protect you from the elements and provide a safe, comfortable living space. A well-built shelter is more than just a place to sleep—it is your primary defense against the challenges of the environment and a foundation for resilience and security in uncertain times.

3.3 Advanced Building Techniques

As you progress beyond basic shelter construction, advanced techniques can significantly improve the durability, sustainability, and comfort of your living space. These methods often stem from traditional practices refined over centuries to maximize local materials and adapt to environmental conditions. By incorporating sustainable materials like earthbags, cob, and straw bales, integrating renewable energy systems, and building communal spaces and infrastructure, you can create a shelter that addresses immediate survival needs while fostering long-term resilience and supporting community development.

Utilizing Sustainable Materials: Earthbags, Cob, and Straw Bales

In a post-collapse world, utilizing materials in ways that minimize environmental impact while maximizing durability and energy efficiency is essential. Three such materials—earthbags, cob, and straw bales—are particularly well-suited for constructing robust, sustainable shelters. These materials can be sourced locally, reducing the need for external resources, and are ideal for creating long-lasting, resilient homes.

Earthbag construction is a versatile and resilient technique that involves filling durable bags, often made of polypropylene or burlap, with earth or other natural materials like sand or gravel, and stacking them to form walls. The bags are tamped down to compress the contents and create strong, load-bearing structures. This method is especially beneficial in areas where wood or stone are scarce but earth is plentiful. Earthbag buildings are incredibly durable, resistant to fire, water, and pests, and offer excellent insulation due to the thermal mass of the earth. They can be shaped into various forms such as domes, arches, or rectangular structures, depending on the design preferences and local environment. While earthbag construction is labor-intensive, it does not require specialized skills, making it an accessible choice for community-based building projects where many hands can help.

Cob construction is another ancient, highly sustainable building method that involves mixing clay, sand, straw, and water to form thick, sculpted walls. The mixture is applied by hand to create monolithic walls that are left to dry and harden. Cob buildings are renowned for their thermal efficiency, as the thick walls retain warmth in cold weather and stay cool in hot weather, reducing the need for external energy sources. Cob is highly sustainable since it uses abundant, renewable materials that can often be sourced directly from the construction site. Cob walls are incredibly strong and durable, often lasting for centuries with proper maintenance, making it ideal for long-term shelter. The flexibility of cob also allows for creative, organic designs that can incorporate built-in furniture, sculpted features, and custom-sized windows and doors.

Straw bale construction is a third sustainable option, especially in regions where straw is readily available as a byproduct of local agriculture. Straw bales are stacked like bricks, secured with wooden or metal pins, and covered with plaster or clay to form thick, insulated walls. The superior insulation properties of straw bale walls make them especially energy-efficient, maintaining warmth in winter and coolness in summer. This makes straw bale construction particularly valuable in regions with extreme temperature fluctuations. The plaster layer protects the straw from moisture and pests, ensuring the durability of the structure. Straw bale buildings can be constructed relatively quickly, and like cob, they offer opportunities for creative design, such as curved walls or large window openings. Additionally, the natural materials used in straw bale construction are biodegradable, further enhancing its environmental benefits.

These three building techniques—earthbags, cob, and straw bales—offer sustainable, energy-efficient, and resilient solutions for shelter construction in a post-collapse world. By utilizing these materials, you can build homes that are not only functional and comfortable but also environmentally friendly and long-lasting.

Incorporating Renewable Energy Systems

In addition to the physical construction of your shelter, incorporating renewable energy systems is crucial for ensuring long-term self-sufficiency. In a post-collapse world, reliance on traditional energy sources such as fossil fuels or grid electricity may no longer be feasible, making renewable energy a vital component of your shelter's design.

Solar energy is one of the most accessible and practical forms of renewable energy, especially in sunny regions. Photovoltaic (PV) panels can be installed on the roof or on the ground to capture sunlight and convert it into electricity, which can be used to power lights, appliances, and other essential devices. Solar water heaters can also be installed to provide hot water for bathing, cooking, and cleaning, reducing the need for fuel-based heating methods. The efficiency of solar energy systems depends on the local climate and the orientation of the panels, so it's important to assess your location's solar potential before installation.

Wind energy is another option, particularly in areas with consistent wind patterns. Small wind turbines can be installed to generate electricity, either as a primary power source or to supplement solar energy systems. Wind turbines can be mounted on rooftops or freestanding poles, and they work best in open areas where the wind is not obstructed by buildings or trees. While wind energy systems can be more complex and costly to install than solar, they provide a valuable alternative or complement to solar power, especially in regions where wind is more reliable than sunlight.

Water power can also be harnessed if your shelter is located near a flowing river or stream. Micro-hydro systems use the kinetic energy of moving water to generate electricity, providing a consistent and renewable power source. These systems are highly efficient and can produce electricity around the clock, unlike solar and wind, which are dependent on weather conditions. However, the installation of a micro-hydro system requires careful planning and engineering to ensure that it does not disrupt the local ecosystem or become damaged by seasonal fluctuations in water flow.

Constructing Communal Buildings and Infrastructure

As your survival community grows, the need for communal buildings and infrastructure will become increasingly important. These structures serve not only as functional spaces for work, storage, and gatherings but also as symbols of the community's resilience and cooperation. Constructing communal buildings requires a collaborative approach, with each member contributing their skills, labor, and resources to the project.

Community halls, **workshops**, and **storage facilities** are among the most critical communal structures. A community hall provides a central meeting place where members can gather for discussions, decision-making, and social events. This building should be large enough to accommodate the entire community and should be constructed with durability and comfort in mind. Workshops are essential for maintaining tools, producing goods, and carrying out repairs. These spaces should be equipped with workbenches, storage for tools and materials, and adequate ventilation and lighting. Storage facilities, such as barns or warehouses, are necessary for storing food, supplies, and equipment. These buildings should be secure, well-ventilated, and protected from pests and weather.

Infrastructure development is also crucial for supporting the needs of the community. This includes creating roads and pathways for easy access to different parts of the community, digging wells or installing water systems for a reliable water supply, and constructing waste management systems such as composting toilets or septic tanks. Building and maintaining this infrastructure requires careful planning and ongoing maintenance to ensure that it meets the community's needs without causing environmental degradation.

In conclusion, advanced building techniques offer a pathway to creating durable, sustainable, and resilient shelters that can support not only individual survival but also the development of a thriving community. By utilizing sustainable materials, incorporating renewable energy systems, and constructing communal buildings and infrastructure, you can create a living environment that is not only functional and protective but also capable of supporting long-term growth and stability in a post-collapse world. These techniques, rooted in both traditional wisdom and modern innovation, provide the tools needed to build a future where self-sufficiency and community resilience are the foundations of survival.

3.4 Maintenance and Repairs

Building a sturdy and sustainable shelter is only the beginning of ensuring long-term survival and comfort in a post-collapse world. Equally important is the ongoing maintenance and repair of your shelter, which ensures it continues to provide reliable protection from the elements, security from potential threats, and a comfortable living environment. Without consistent upkeep, even the most robustly constructed shelter will gradually deteriorate, creating vulnerabilities that could become life-threatening. This section will delve into the importance of establishing regular inspection routines, identifying common issues that may arise, exploring DIY repair techniques, and implementing strategies for gradually upgrading your shelter as time goes on. By prioritizing maintenance, you can extend the lifespan of your shelter, maintain its efficiency, and adapt it to meet the evolving needs of your survival.

Regular Inspection Routines

The foundation of effective shelter maintenance lies in regular inspections. A consistent, systematic approach to inspecting your shelter enables you to spot and address potential problems before they grow into significant issues. Inspections should be performed at least seasonally, with additional checks following major weather events such as storms, heavy rains, or extreme temperatures that could affect the integrity of your shelter.

Start each inspection by thoroughly evaluating the roof, which serves as your primary defense against the elements. Any damage to the roof can lead to leaks, water damage, and weakened structural stability. Look for missing or damaged shingles, tiles, or other roofing materials. If the roof is made of thatch or metal, check for signs of wear, rust, or degradation. Pay close attention to the areas around chimneys, vents, and skylights, as these are common entry points for water. Clear away any debris such as leaves, branches, or dirt, as these can trap moisture and speed up deterioration.

Next, inspect the walls, both on the interior and exterior. Look for cracks, holes, or gaps in the structure that could allow water, wind, or pests to infiltrate. Be particularly mindful of the areas around windows and doors, where the sealant or caulking might have broken down over time. If your walls are made of wood, check for signs of rot, insect damage, or warping. For stone or earth walls, look for loose or crumbling sections that may require reinforcement. On the interior, watch for indications of mold, mildew, or dampness, as these may signal leaks or insufficient ventilation.

The foundation is another critical area to assess. A stable foundation is essential for the overall stability of your shelter, and any issues here can quickly lead to more serious structural problems. Look for cracks, uneven settling, or signs of erosion or water pooling around the base of the shelter. If the structure is built on stilts or piers, examine them for signs of wood rot or weakening, which could compromise the shelter's safety.

Finally, don't forget the doors and windows. These are not only entry points for people but also for air, water, and pests. Ensure that all doors and windows open and close smoothly, the seals are intact, and there are no gaps or cracks around the frames. Check that locks and latches are functional and secure, providing sufficient protection against intruders. Regular attention to these areas will help maintain the safety, comfort, and long-term viability of your shelter.

Common Issues and DIY Repair Techniques

Even with regular maintenance, issues will inevitably arise that require attention. Being prepared with the knowledge and tools to handle common repairs can save time, resources, and potentially prevent larger problems.

Leaks and water damage are among the most common issues in any shelter. If you notice water stains on the ceiling or walls, act quickly to locate and repair the source of the leak. For small leaks in the roof, applying roofing cement or sealant to the affected area may be sufficient. For larger issues, you may need to replace damaged shingles or sections of the roof entirely. Inside the shelter, remove any damaged materials, such as drywall or insulation, that have been compromised by water, and ensure the area is thoroughly dried before making repairs to prevent mold growth.

Rot and insect damage in wood structures are also common, particularly in damp or humid environments. If you identify rot, cut out the affected section and replace it with new wood, treating the area with a preservative to prevent further decay. For insect damage, such as from termites or carpenter ants, it's important to eliminate the source of the infestation and treat the wood with insecticides or natural deterrents, like borax, to protect the structure.

Cracks in walls or foundations can be a sign of settling or shifting in your shelter. Small cracks can often be filled with mortar or caulk to prevent them from widening. However, larger cracks may indicate a more serious structural issue that requires reinforcement, such as adding support beams or underpinning the foundation. In earth-based structures, like cob or adobe, cracks can often be repaired by reapplying the original mixture and blending it into the surrounding wall.

Pest infestations are another challenge that can compromise the integrity of your shelter. Rodents, insects, and other pests can cause significant damage if left unchecked. Regularly inspect your shelter for signs of pests, such as droppings, nests, or gnaw marks. Seal any potential entry points, such as gaps in walls or around doors and windows, and consider setting traps or using natural repellents, like peppermint oil or diatomaceous earth, to deter pests.

Strategies for Upgrading Your Shelter Over Time

As your shelter ages and your needs evolve, it may be necessary to upgrade or enhance your living space. These upgrades can range from improving insulation and energy efficiency to expanding the size of your shelter to accommodate more people or activities.

One of the most impactful upgrades you can make is improving **insulation**. As mentioned earlier, natural materials like straw, wool, or earth can provide excellent insulation, but as resources allow, you may consider adding modern insulation materials, such as foam boards or reflective barriers, to further improve your shelter's thermal performance. Proper insulation not only makes your shelter more comfortable but also reduces the amount of fuel needed for heating and cooling, which is crucial in a resource-scarce environment.

Another upgrade to consider is the addition of **renewable energy systems**, such as solar panels, wind turbines, or micro-hydro generators. These systems can provide reliable electricity for lighting, heating, and powering essential devices, making your shelter more self-sufficient and less reliant on external resources. Even small-scale systems can make a significant difference in your daily life and contribute to the long-term sustainability of your shelter.

Expanding your shelter may become necessary as your community grows or as you accumulate more supplies and equipment. When planning an expansion, ensure that any additions are structurally sound and integrated with the existing shelter. Consider how the expansion will impact the overall layout and functionality of your living space, and plan for additional insulation, ventilation, and waterproofing as needed.

Finally, **modernizing infrastructure** within your shelter, such as improving water collection and filtration systems, upgrading waste management solutions, or enhancing food storage capabilities, can greatly increase the efficiency and comfort of your living space. These upgrades not only improve your quality of life but also help to future-proof your shelter against changing conditions and needs.

In conclusion, regular maintenance and repairs are essential for the long-term viability of your shelter. By establishing consistent inspection routines, addressing common issues promptly, and strategically upgrading your shelter over time, you can ensure that your living space remains safe, secure, and comfortable in the face of an uncertain future. The effort you invest in maintaining and improving your shelter will pay off in increased resilience, security, and sustainability for years to come.

Chapter 4: Adapting to a Changing Climate

As the post-collapse world reshapes itself, the growing reality of climate change demands innovative solutions. Adaptation isn't just about surviving today—it's about thriving in the new normal while preparing for an unpredictable future. This chapter explores strategies for resilience, sustainability, and the integration of natural systems into human survival frameworks.

4.1 Building Resilient Communities Against Climate Shocks

The collapse has left communities vulnerable to climate extremes: rising temperatures, erratic weather patterns, and intensified natural disasters. Rebuilding civilization must prioritize climate resilience, which ensures that communities can withstand shocks like floods, droughts, and heatwaves without collapsing again. Resilient communities are proactive, not reactive—they anticipate challenges and adapt before disaster strikes.

Core Principles of Resilient Communities

1. **Diversified Livelihoods:** Encourage multi-source income and food production. Combining farming, fishing, and trade creates redundancy, minimizing risk if one sector fails.
2. **Collaborative Networks:** Communities must rely on collective action, pooling resources and expertise to face

challenges like rebuilding water systems or managing shared energy sources.
3. **Infrastructure Design:** Adopt building techniques and materials that can withstand local climate risks. In flood-prone regions, for instance, stilted homes and water-resistant materials become critical.

Steps to Build Resilience

1. Risk Assessment and Mapping

- Identify climate risks specific to your region. Tools like community mapping can help visualize vulnerabilities (e.g., flood-prone areas, heat zones).
- Involve everyone in the community to ensure comprehensive coverage, from elders who remember historical trends to youth who can bring new perspectives.

2. Community Shelters and Safe Zones

- Designate areas that can serve as emergency shelters during disasters. Ensure they are strategically located, accessible, and stocked with essentials like food, water, and first-aid supplies.
- Construct safe zones with multipurpose use, such as storm shelters doubling as communal storage facilities.

3. Localized Early Warning Systems

- Establish low-tech warning systems, like watchtowers or flags, to signal impending disasters.
- Train community members in weather monitoring using barometers, thermometers, and pattern recognition.

4. Water and Food Security Plans

- Build rainwater harvesting systems to ensure year-round water access.
- Develop food storage systems, such as underground root cellars or community granaries, to secure supplies during lean periods.

4.2 Living Sustainably in a Changed Environment

The collapse of traditional systems has left humanity at a crossroads, offering an opportunity to build a new way of life that harmonizes with the environment. Living sustainably in a changed world requires a shift in mindset, focusing on self-reliance, resource conservation, and systems that regenerate rather than deplete. This approach is not merely about survival—it is about creating a lifestyle that can endure for generations, ensuring both human prosperity and ecological balance.

Adapting to Local Resources

In a post-collapse world, the environment dictates what resources are available and how they should be used. Sustainable living starts with understanding the local ecosystem and its limitations. For instance, in arid regions, water conservation becomes paramount, while areas with abundant rainfall might focus on flood management and soil preservation. Communities must learn to live within the carrying capacity of their surroundings, avoiding practices that degrade or exhaust natural resources.

One of the most critical steps is localizing food production. By growing food suited to the environment, such as drought-resistant crops in dry regions or water-intensive crops where water is plentiful, communities can reduce reliance on external sources. Techniques like companion planting, which pairs plants that support each other's growth, and crop rotation, which preserves soil health, are essential for long-term agricultural success. Similarly, integrating livestock and crop systems can create a closed-loop cycle where waste from one serves as an input for the other.

Energy Conservation and Renewables

Energy use must also align with sustainability goals. Fossil fuels and other non-renewable energy sources are no longer viable options in a post-collapse context. Instead, communities must adopt renewable energy systems tailored to their environment. Solar panels can provide electricity in sunny regions, while wind turbines are better suited to areas with consistent winds. Hydropower, even at a micro scale, can be a reliable option near rivers or streams.

Beyond generating power, conserving energy is equally vital. Passive design principles can make homes more energy-efficient by maximizing natural light, ventilation, and insulation. For example, positioning homes to capture the sun's heat during winter and shade during summer reduces the need for artificial heating and cooling. Additionally, tools and appliances that rely on manual or solar power, such as solar cookers or hand-cranked devices, further reduce energy demands.

Closing the Loop with Waste Management

Sustainable living requires a fundamental rethinking of waste. In a regenerative system, waste is not discarded but repurposed as a resource. Organic waste, such as food scraps and plant material, can be composted to create nutrient-rich soil for farming. Greywater—wastewater from sinks, baths, and laundry—can be filtered through natural systems, such as gravel beds or constructed wetlands, and reused for irrigation.

Communities must also address the challenges of managing non-organic waste. Recycling and repurposing materials like metal, glass, and plastic help reduce environmental pollution and extend the lifecycle of finite resources. For instance, broken tools can be repaired or salvaged for parts, while discarded containers can serve as storage solutions or planting pots. This circular approach minimizes waste and fosters innovation in resource use.

Cultural and Behavioral Shifts

Sustainability is as much a cultural shift as it is a technical one. Communities must embrace a mindset of sufficiency—prioritizing needs over wants and focusing on quality over quantity. This requires a departure from the consumerist values of pre-collapse society, replacing them with practices that value resourcefulness, repair, and reuse.

Education plays a crucial role in fostering this mindset. Teaching practical skills, such as food preservation, water purification, and natural building techniques, equips individuals to live independently while contributing to the community. Shared knowledge, passed through workshops or oral tradition, strengthens communal bonds and ensures that critical skills are preserved.

Celebrating sustainability through cultural practices can also reinforce its importance. Festivals, rituals, and storytelling centered on the themes of nature and regeneration can inspire collective action. For example, harvest festivals can highlight the importance of sustainable farming, while tree-planting ceremonies can instill a sense of stewardship for the environment.

Balancing Growth and Preservation

Sustainable living does not mean rejecting progress but aligning it with ecological principles. Communities should aim for balanced growth, where advancements in technology and infrastructure complement, rather than disrupt, natural systems. For example, incorporating green roofs and walls into urban environments can provide insulation, reduce heat islands, and support biodiversity. Similarly, designing transportation systems around walking, cycling, and public transit reduces energy consumption and minimizes environmental impact.

Preservation must remain at the core of all development efforts. Protecting forests, wetlands, and other critical ecosystems safeguards the services they provide, from clean water and air to climate regulation. These natural systems are not just resources to be used but partners in creating a sustainable future.

A New Way Forward

Living sustainably in a changed environment is about more than adapting to new circumstances—it is about thriving within them. By aligning human systems with the natural world, communities can create a way of life that is resilient, regenerative, and fulfilling. This new way forward requires effort, creativity, and a collective commitment to stewardship, but it offers the promise of a better, more sustainable future.

4.3 Harnessing Nature to Mitigate Future Risks

Nature offers humanity a partner in its efforts to rebuild after a collapse. By understanding and utilizing the natural systems already in place, communities can mitigate future risks while fostering environmental restoration. This approach is not only practical but also essential for long-term resilience, as it integrates ecological balance with human survival strategies. The interplay between human ingenuity and the natural world can yield powerful solutions, from stabilizing coastlines to restoring forests and creating biodiverse landscapes.

Forests, for instance, are among nature's most valuable tools for mitigating climate risks. Acting as carbon sinks, they absorb excess carbon dioxide, slow the pace of climate change, and stabilize soil against erosion. Communities rebuilding after a collapse should prioritize reforestation efforts, focusing on degraded or deforested areas. Agroforestry, a system that integrates trees and crops, provides additional benefits by creating diverse, productive landscapes. Trees protect crops from extreme weather, enrich the soil with organic matter, and offer a renewable source of food, fuel, and building materials. Such systems also enhance biodiversity, allowing ecosystems to recover and thrive alongside human activity.

Coastal and riverine areas present unique challenges and opportunities for using nature as a defense mechanism. Coastal mangrove forests, for example, act as buffers against storm surges and tsunamis. Their dense root systems stabilize the shoreline, reducing erosion while providing habitats for aquatic species that sustain local food systems. Similarly, wetlands serve as natural sponges, absorbing floodwaters and filtering pollutants, making them invaluable in flood-prone regions. Restoring these ecosystems not only minimizes the impact of extreme weather events but also enhances water quality and supports local biodiversity. In addition, living shorelines—comprising oyster reefs, native grasses, and other natural elements—offer an alternative to artificial barriers like concrete seawalls. These systems evolve and adapt over time, providing sustainable protection against coastal erosion.

Soil conservation and regenerative agricultural practices also play a critical role in mitigating risks. Healthy soils act as carbon reservoirs, sequestering greenhouse gases while retaining moisture and nutrients essential for plant growth. Techniques such as cover cropping, no-till farming, and composting improve soil structure and fertility, ensuring long-term productivity. In regions with steep slopes, terracing can reduce water runoff and prevent soil loss, while vetiver grass hedges offer natural barriers to erosion. These approaches not only secure food supplies but also stabilize the landscape against environmental shocks.

Urban environments, too, can benefit from harnessing nature. Urban greening initiatives, such as planting trees along streets, creating rooftop gardens, and building urban forests, help counteract the heat island effect caused by concrete and asphalt. These efforts reduce temperatures, improve air quality, and provide recreational spaces for residents. Green roofs, in particular, offer a dual advantage: they insulate buildings, reducing energy consumption, and manage stormwater, lessening the risk of urban flooding. Community gardens can further enhance urban resilience, providing fresh produce while fostering a sense of collective purpose.

The success of nature-based solutions depends on community involvement. Engaging local populations in reforestation, wetland restoration, or urban greening projects ensures that these initiatives are tailored to regional needs and have widespread support. Educating younger generations about the value of ecosystems and the principles of environmental stewardship can cultivate a lasting commitment to sustainability. Similarly, traditional ecological knowledge, often held by indigenous communities, can offer time-tested strategies for managing natural resources and responding to environmental challenges.

By aligning human efforts with natural processes, communities can create resilient systems that not only withstand future risks but also enhance the health of the planet. Harnessing nature is a reminder that survival and prosperity are most assured when humanity works in harmony with the environment.

4.4 Preparing for Long-Term Environmental Challenges

While short-term adaptation is crucial for immediate survival, the greatest test for post-collapse societies lies in preparing for long-term environmental challenges. Climate change, biodiversity loss, and resource scarcity are not temporary crises—they represent fundamental shifts that demand a rethinking of how societies interact with the environment. Building systems that can endure these changes requires foresight, innovation, and a commitment to sustainability.

One of the most pressing challenges is the increasing frequency and severity of extreme weather events. Floods, droughts, hurricanes, and heatwaves are already reshaping landscapes and disrupting livelihoods. To address these risks, communities must invest in robust infrastructure designed for resilience. Flood-resistant buildings, elevated foundations, and heat-reflective materials are examples of architectural adaptations that can protect lives and assets. In drought-prone areas, water-efficient landscaping, such as xeriscaping, reduces reliance on irrigation by using native, drought-tolerant plants.

Food security is another cornerstone of long-term resilience. Climate change will alter growing seasons, rainfall patterns, and pest dynamics, requiring a shift toward climate-resilient agriculture. Farmers must embrace crop varieties adapted to their changing environments, such as salt-tolerant crops in coastal areas or heat-resistant grains in arid zones. Seed banks, which preserve a diverse array of plant genetics, are vital resources for ensuring future agricultural stability. These banks provide access to traditional crop varieties that have evolved to thrive under specific environmental conditions. In addition, aquaculture can supplement terrestrial food systems, offering a reliable source of protein through fish farms or integrated aquaponics systems.

Water management is another critical area of focus. As precipitation patterns shift, some regions will face water scarcity while others experience flooding. Integrated water resource management (IWRM) offers a holistic approach to balancing water needs across agricultural, industrial, and domestic sectors. Techniques such as groundwater recharge, rainwater harvesting, and efficient irrigation systems can maximize water availability while minimizing waste. Desalination technologies, powered by renewable energy, provide a solution for arid coastal areas where freshwater is scarce.

Biodiversity conservation is equally essential for long-term resilience. Healthy ecosystems support services that humans rely on, from pollination and pest control to carbon storage and water purification. Establishing wildlife corridors—stretches of natural habitat that connect fragmented ecosystems—allows species to migrate, adapt, and maintain genetic diversity. Protecting pollinators, such as bees and butterflies, ensures the continued production of many crops. Conservation efforts should also include community-managed protected areas, where local populations play a central role in safeguarding biodiversity.

Education and training are critical to equipping communities with the skills needed to adapt to environmental challenges. Workshops on permaculture, water conservation, and sustainable building techniques can empower individuals to contribute meaningfully to their communities' resilience. Lifelong learning programs ensure that knowledge evolves alongside environmental conditions, enabling societies to respond to emerging threats.

Collaboration between neighboring communities enhances the effectiveness of adaptation efforts. Regional partnerships can facilitate the sharing of resources, knowledge, and best practices, creating a network of support that extends beyond individual settlements. Coordinated disaster response plans, for example, can save lives and resources during emergencies. Monitoring systems, managed by local teams, can track environmental changes such as rainfall, temperature, or soil quality, providing the data needed to refine adaptation strategies over time.

Preparing for the worst-case scenarios—mass migrations, uninhabitable regions, or ecosystem collapse—requires flexible and forward-thinking solutions. Communities should identify potential safe zones and establish migration pathways to ensure orderly relocation if necessary. Stockpiling critical resources, such as seeds, medicines, and tools, provides a buffer against future disruptions. At the same time, fostering connections with distant regions or nations can enable the exchange of innovations and mutual support during crises.

Ultimately, the goal of long-term preparation is not merely to survive but to thrive in a world transformed by environmental challenges. By embracing adaptation, innovation, and collaboration, post-collapse societies can build a future that is not only resilient but also sustainable, equitable, and in harmony with the natural world.

Chapter 5: Water Management and Sanitation

Water is essential for life, and maintaining proper sanitation is equally critical to safeguarding health. In a post-collapse world, effective management of water resources and hygiene practices becomes paramount to prevent disease outbreaks and promote the well-being of a community. This chapter offers practical, actionable solutions for efficiently managing water supplies, ensuring clean and safe water for drinking, cooking, and hygiene purposes. It also explores strategies for maintaining sanitation through waste management systems that prevent contamination and protect the health of the population. By implementing these strategies, communities can not only survive but thrive, minimizing the risks of illness and ensuring long-term health and stability.

5.1 Finding and Purifying Water

In any scenario where civilization has collapsed or resources are scarce, access to clean, safe water becomes absolutely essential. Water is not just a basic necessity for survival; it is the very foundation upon which life depends. Understanding how to locate water sources and purify them is crucial knowledge that every individual must possess, especially when rebuilding or maintaining a community. Without water, survival becomes increasingly difficult, making the ability to find, purify, and manage water a core skill in any survivalist's toolkit.

When you find yourself in the wild or an environment where established water systems are no longer functional, the first task is to locate a viable water source. Streams, rivers, lakes, and even dew on plants can all be potential sources of water. In arid regions, natural depressions can trap water after rainfall, and digging near dry riverbeds often reveals water just below the surface. Additionally, certain plants, such as bamboo or the base of cacti, can be tapped for water. However, these methods require a good understanding of the environment and the proper techniques, as not all water sources are safe to drink directly.

Once you've identified a potential water source, the next critical step is purification. Even water that appears clean can harbor pathogens that cause serious, life-threatening diseases. Boiling is the most reliable method of purification. Bringing water to a rolling boil for at least one minute (or three minutes at higher altitudes) kills most bacteria, viruses, and parasites. However, boiling requires both a heat source and a container, which may not always be readily available. In such cases, filtration offers a practical alternative.

Filtration methods vary from simple, homemade systems to more advanced portable filters. A basic yet effective technique involves using a cloth to filter out larger particles, followed by a homemade filter consisting of layers of sand, charcoal, and gravel in a container to remove smaller contaminants. Commercial portable water filters, which are lightweight and specifically designed for emergency situations, can eliminate up to 99.9% of harmful pathogens. Another method is chemical treatment using iodine tablets or chlorine drops, which effectively neutralize harmful microorganisms. However, these chemicals can leave an unpleasant taste and may not be as effective against certain parasites.

In addition to boiling and filtration, setting up a rainwater collection system is an excellent way to secure a renewable water supply, particularly in regions with regular rainfall. This system can be as simple as placing containers under natural runoff points or constructing a more elaborate setup with gutters, pipes, and storage tanks to capture and store rainwater. While rainwater is generally safer than ground or surface water, it still requires filtration and possibly chemical treatment to ensure it is safe for drinking. By mastering these purification and collection techniques, you not only secure access to one of the most vital resources on Earth but also build resilience, ensuring that your community can weather future crises and challenges.

5.2. Building Water Systems

Beyond locating and purifying water, the next critical step in ensuring long-term survival is the construction of a reliable water system capable of sustainably meeting your needs. Establishing infrastructure such as wells, cisterns, and gravity-fed systems are foundational projects that can ensure a stable water supply for drinking, agriculture, and sanitation. These systems, when properly designed and maintained, provide the resilience necessary to support both individual and community needs in the face of uncertain resources.

Building a well is one of the most effective ways to access groundwater, which is often less contaminated than surface water. Depending on the depth of the water table, wells can be either hand-dug or drilled. Hand-dug wells, although labor-intensive, can be a viable option in areas where the water table is shallow and accessible. The process involves digging a wide shaft and lining it with stones, bricks, or concrete to prevent the structure from collapsing and to protect the water from surface contamination. For deeper water tables, drilling becomes necessary, requiring specialized equipment to bore a narrow hole deep into the earth. Once completed, it's crucial to protect the well from surface contaminants by constructing a sturdy cover and ensuring the surrounding area is maintained and kept clean.

Cisterns are another vital system designed to collect and store rainwater or surface runoff. These can be built both above or below ground, with materials ranging from concrete and stone to more modern options like plastic. The essential factor in an effective cistern is ensuring it is well-sealed to prevent contamination and includes a filtration system to purify the water before it is used for drinking or other purposes. Cisterns can serve as a critical backup water source during dry spells or in places where other water supplies are unreliable or unavailable.

Designing a gravity-fed water system is another critical skill, especially when supplying water for agricultural purposes or providing water to a larger community. Gravity-fed systems utilize the natural slope of the land to move water from a higher elevation to where it is needed, eliminating the need for pumps and making the system more energy-efficient. The process involves setting up a reservoir at a higher point on the landscape and directing the water downhill through pipes or channels. These systems can provide a steady flow of water for irrigation, supporting crops, or even for supplying homes, provided the topography of the land permits.

By understanding and implementing these water systems, you not only secure a sustainable and reliable water supply but also promote long-term sustainability. These methods are designed to be low-maintenance and depend on readily available materials, making them viable even in environments with limited resources. By establishing wells, cisterns, and gravity-fed systems, you lay the foundation for a resilient community that is capable of thriving independently of external systems, ultimately ensuring access to vital water resources for the future.

5.3 Waste Management and Sanitation

The importance of waste management and sanitation in a post-collapse environment cannot be overstated. In scenarios where modern plumbing and waste disposal systems have ceased to function, communities must adopt sustainable practices to manage human waste and other refuse. Poor sanitation is one of the quickest routes to the outbreak of diseases such as cholera, dysentery, and typhoid, which can spread rapidly in crowded, resource-limited settings. Therefore, implementing effective waste management and sanitation systems is not just a matter of maintaining comfort but is essential for preserving the health and well-being of the community.

One of the most practical solutions for managing human waste in a grid-down scenario is the use of composting toilets. Unlike conventional flush toilets, composting toilets do not require a continuous supply of water, making them ideal for off-grid living. These systems operate by separating liquid and solid waste, with the latter being broken down by aerobic bacteria into a stable, non-toxic compost. Constructing a composting toilet can be done with basic materials: a sturdy wooden structure for privacy, a collection chamber for waste, and a ventilation system to minimize odors and facilitate aerobic decomposition. The use of carbon-rich materials such as sawdust, straw, or dry leaves is critical in balancing the nitrogen content of human waste, thus accelerating the composting process and preventing foul smells.

The compost produced by these toilets can, after sufficient decomposition, be safely used to enrich soil for non-edible plants or even for edible crops in some cases, provided it is adequately processed. This approach not only addresses waste disposal but also contributes to the sustainability of the community by closing the nutrient loop and enhancing soil fertility. However, it is crucial to follow best practices in compost management, such as ensuring the composting process reaches temperatures high enough to kill pathogens, and allowing the compost to cure for several months before use. This not only ensures safety but also maximizes the nutrient value of the compost.

Beyond human waste, managing greywater—water that comes from sinks, showers, and laundry—plays a vital role in maintaining hygiene and preventing environmental contamination. Unlike blackwater, greywater contains fewer pathogens and can be treated and reused for irrigation or flushing toilets. Designing a greywater system requires careful planning to avoid contamination and ensure that the water is safely reused. Simple greywater systems can involve diverting water through a gravel and sand filter, where it can be further purified by plants in a constructed wetland or mulch basin. These natural filtration systems are highly effective and sustainable, requiring minimal maintenance while providing essential irrigation for gardens or agricultural areas.

More advanced greywater systems can include multiple stages of filtration and treatment, such as using biochar or activated carbon to remove chemical contaminants, or employing aerobic treatment units to further break down organic matter. These systems are scalable depending on the size of the community and the available resources. By effectively treating and reusing greywater, a community can significantly reduce its demand for fresh water, making it a critical component of any water management strategy in a resource-constrained environment.

Additionally, the prevention of contamination is paramount in any waste management and sanitation strategy. This involves not only the proper construction and placement of latrines and composting systems but also the education and enforcement of strict hygiene practices. Latrines should be located at least 200 feet away from water sources and on lower ground to prevent runoff from contaminating the community's water supply. Regular handwashing, particularly after using the toilet and before handling food, should be rigorously enforced. In a situation where medical facilities may be limited or non-existent, preventing the spread of disease through proper waste management and sanitation is crucial for the survival of the community.

Moreover, communities must establish protocols for the disposal of non-organic waste, such as plastics and metals, which can accumulate and pose environmental hazards. In the absence of formal waste disposal systems, recycling and reusing materials becomes not only a practical solution but a necessity. Scrap metals can be repurposed for tools and construction, while plastics can be used for insulation or waterproofing. Organic waste, aside from human excrement, can be composted to create additional fertilizer for crops, further enhancing the sustainability of the community.

In conclusion, waste management and sanitation are not merely logistical concerns but are fundamental to the survival and health of a post-collapse society. Through the use of composting toilets, greywater systems, and strict hygiene practices, communities can mitigate the risks associated with poor sanitation, prevent the outbreak of disease, and create a sustainable environment that supports long-term survival and growth. These practices, while simple, require diligent implementation and maintenance to ensure their effectiveness, making them a critical component of any survival strategy.

5.4 Community Water Infrastructure

As the scale of survival efforts increases from individuals and small groups to larger communities, the complexity and importance of water management grow exponentially. Building and maintaining a robust community water infrastructure is crucial not only for ensuring access to safe drinking water but also for supporting agricultural activities, sanitation, and overall public health. A well-designed water infrastructure enables a community to thrive even in the most challenging circumstances, making it a foundational element of any long-term survival plan.

The first step in developing community water infrastructure is a comprehensive assessment of the community's water needs and available resources. This includes identifying potential water sources, such as rivers, lakes, underground aquifers, or rainwater, and determining their capacity to meet the community's needs. It is essential to consider both current and future water demands, accounting for population growth, agricultural expansion, and seasonal variations in water availability. This assessment should also include an evaluation of the local geography and climate, which will influence the design and placement of water infrastructure.

Once the assessment is complete, the next phase involves designing a water distribution system that ensures equitable access to all members of the community. This system might include a combination of wells, cisterns, reservoirs, and pipelines. For instance, a central reservoir can be constructed to store water from multiple sources, which is then distributed through a network of gravity-fed pipelines to various parts of the community. Gravity-fed systems are particularly advantageous in off-grid scenarios because they require no external power source, relying instead on the natural gradient of the land to move water from higher to lower elevations. These systems are not only efficient but also relatively easy to maintain, making them ideal for long-term use.

In addition to ensuring equitable distribution, it is crucial to establish protocols for the sustainable use and management of water resources. This includes implementing water-saving techniques, such as drip irrigation for agriculture, which minimizes water loss due to evaporation and runoff. Communities should also prioritize the protection of water sources from contamination. This can be achieved by designating protected areas around wells and reservoirs, preventing the use of harmful chemicals in nearby agricultural practices, and educating the community about the importance of safeguarding their water supply.

Maintaining the infrastructure is another critical aspect of community water management. This involves regular inspections of wells, pipelines, and storage tanks to detect and repair leaks or other damage promptly. In a post-collapse scenario, where access to materials and skilled labor may be limited, it is vital to train members of the community in basic maintenance and repair techniques. By creating a team responsible for the upkeep of water infrastructure, communities can ensure that their water supply remains reliable and safe over the long term.

Furthermore, community involvement in water management is essential for the success of these systems. Establishing a water committee or cooperative can help manage the distribution of water, resolve disputes, and coordinate maintenance efforts. Such a committee should represent all sectors of the community, ensuring that the needs and concerns of all members are addressed. In times of scarcity, these committees can also implement rationing systems to ensure that water is distributed fairly and that essential needs, such as drinking and sanitation, are prioritized.

Lastly, communities must prepare for emergencies, such as droughts or contamination incidents, that could disrupt the water supply. This requires having contingency plans in place, such as alternative water sources, emergency storage tanks, and purification methods. Communities might also invest in technologies that allow for the rapid deployment of additional water resources, such as portable desalination units or mobile water purification systems. In addition, stockpiling water purification tablets and training community members in their use can provide a crucial backup in the event of an emergency.

In conclusion, building a community water infrastructure is a complex but essential task that requires careful planning, sustainable management, and ongoing maintenance. By ensuring that all members of the community have access to clean, safe water, and by preparing for potential disruptions, communities can build resilience and increase their chances of survival in the long term. Water is the lifeblood of any society, and in a post-collapse world, it will be the cornerstone upon which a new civilization is built. The successful management of this resource will not only sustain life but will also enable communities to thrive and grow, even in the most challenging environments.

Chapter 6: Reestablishing Communication and Transportation

Reconnecting with others is crucial for survival and stability in a post-collapse world. In such challenging times, rebuilding communication and transportation networks becomes essential to ensure that you can stay connected, share resources, and coordinate efforts effectively with neighboring communities. This chapter provides a comprehensive approach to restoring these vital systems, outlining strategies for establishing reliable communication channels, re-establishing safe and efficient transportation routes, and fostering collaboration between communities. By rebuilding these networks, you create the foundation for mutual support, resource sharing, and collective problem-solving, which are key to long-term resilience and recovery in a fractured world.

6.1 Emergency Communication Systems

In the aftermath of a societal collapse or disaster, one of the most significant challenges that communities will face is the loss of reliable communication systems. Effective communication, both within the community and with the outside world, is crucial for coordinating relief efforts, ensuring safety, and sharing vital information. As modern communication networks—such as the internet, mobile phones, and landlines—fail, it becomes essential to return to more basic, yet reliable, methods of communication. Quickly and efficiently reestablishing these systems can mean the difference between chaos and order during the critical early stages of recovery.

One of the most practical and accessible forms of emergency communication is the use of radios. Basic radio operation and maintenance skills become invaluable in a grid-down scenario. Hand-crank or battery-operated radios, particularly those using shortwave or HAM frequencies, allow communities to receive important information from outside the immediate area, such as weather updates, news from other communities, and emergency broadcasts. Operating a radio is relatively straightforward but requires practice and familiarity with the equipment. Essential skills include tuning to the correct frequencies, understanding radio etiquette, and maintaining the equipment, which involves regular checks on batteries and antennas to ensure the system remains functional.

In addition to receiving outside information, establishing a local communication network within the community is critical. Distributing handheld radios to key members of the community, such as leaders, security personnel, and medical teams, can facilitate communication across large distances. Radios operating on a shared frequency enable real-time communication, which is vital when immediate action is required. To maintain an organized network, a communication schedule or protocol should be established, ensuring that messages are relayed efficiently and without confusion. In situations where privacy is a concern, coded language or pre-agreed phrases can help protect sensitive information from being intercepted by others.

Another important aspect of emergency communication is the use of non-verbal methods, such as Morse code, which can be transmitted via light, sound, or radio. Morse code is a simple, effective way to communicate when voice transmission isn't feasible due to distance, environmental noise, or the need for discretion. Learning the basics of Morse code is relatively easy and can be an invaluable tool in a survival situation. For example, tapping out messages on a metal surface, flashing a light in a specific pattern, or sending short bursts of radio pulses can all convey messages discreetly over long distances. Communities can establish standard Morse code practices, ensuring that everyone is familiar with the common codes and signals.

Beyond Morse code, there are several other non-verbal communication methods to consider. Signal flags, for instance, can be used for long-range communication, especially in open areas where visibility is clear. Hand signals are essential in situations where silence is crucial, such as during security operations or while hunting. Written messages, although slower than other methods, are useful for delivering detailed instructions or communicating with someone in another part of the community. These messages can be left in designated areas for trusted individuals to pick up or delivered directly by hand.

Redundancy in communication systems is essential for reliability, particularly in survival situations. By integrating multiple methods—such as radios, Morse code, signal flags, and hand signals—communities can ensure they remain connected even if one system fails. The key to effective communication lies in thoughtful planning, training, and regular practice. Communities should conduct drills to familiarize everyone with the equipment, ensure that protocols are understood, and develop the ability to operate effectively under stress. By establishing a comprehensive emergency communication system, communities not only increase their resilience but also improve their ability to coordinate efforts, share resources, and protect their members during times of crisis.

6.2 Rebuilding Transportation Networks

Transportation is a critical element of survival and recovery in a post-collapse environment. As the intricate networks of highways, railways, and public transit systems become damaged or completely non-functional, the ability to move people, goods, and resources within and between communities presents a significant challenge. Rebuilding transportation networks is crucial not only for ensuring the steady flow of essential supplies, but also for enabling medical aid, facilitating communication, and supporting the mobility of the population. In a world without modern vehicles and infrastructure, communities must turn to alternative transportation methods and prioritize the maintenance of their roadways to sustain daily operations and ensure long-term recovery.

The first step in rebuilding transportation systems is clearing and maintaining existing roads. In many cases, roadways may be blocked by debris, overgrown vegetation, or damage caused by natural disasters. Clearing these roads is a labor-intensive process, but it is absolutely essential for restoring basic transportation. Communities should organize work crews to methodically clear the major routes, focusing initially on those that connect vital locations such as food storage areas, medical facilities, and water sources. This process may involve removing fallen trees, repairing potholes, and reinforcing sections of the road that are at risk of further damage. Basic tools, such as shovels, axes, and wheelbarrows, can be extremely helpful, although if available, heavier equipment can greatly speed up the process.

Once the roads are cleared, it's important to implement a regular maintenance schedule. Without ongoing upkeep, even newly cleared roads can become impassable, particularly in areas prone to flooding or landslides. Communities should designate individuals or teams to conduct regular inspections of the roads and make repairs as needed. In addition to physical labor, having a basic understanding of engineering principles, such as drainage patterns to prevent water damage or methods for reinforcing bridges and culverts, can greatly improve the longevity of the infrastructure. In cases where advanced materials are unavailable, creative uses of local resources, such as reinforcing roadbeds with stones or logs, can help ensure the roads remain functional for an extended period.

Alongside road maintenance, alternative transportation methods must be developed to adapt to the limitations of a post-collapse environment. With fuel likely to be in short supply or unavailable altogether, the reliance on motor vehicles will decrease. Bicycles, for instance, become an incredibly useful mode of transportation due to their efficiency, ease of maintenance, and ability to navigate various types of terrain. Communities should encourage the use of bicycles for short to medium-distance travel and set up repair stations where people can maintain and fix their bikes using scavenged parts or basic tools. Offering workshops on bicycle maintenance, such as repairing flat tires or adjusting brakes, will empower community members to keep their bicycles in good working order.

In addition to bicycles, carts and wagons drawn by humans or animals provide a practical solution for transporting heavier loads, such as food, building materials, or water. These carts can be constructed or repurposed from wood, metal, and other available materials. The carts can be designed for specific tasks, such as mobile water tanks or supply wagons, and can be pulled by hand or by animals like horses, donkeys, or oxen, if available. Establishing designated routes for these carts will help streamline transportation within the community, reducing congestion and ensuring that essential goods are efficiently delivered.

Rebuilding transportation networks also involves setting up a community transport system. In larger or more spread-out communities, organizing a system for the regular movement of people and goods becomes essential. This could involve scheduling regular trips between critical locations such as markets, medical centers, and communal kitchens. Volunteers or designated transport coordinators can help manage this system, ensuring that resources are available to everyone. For longer distances or more difficult terrain, solutions like constructing simple rail carts on abandoned railway tracks or utilizing waterways, where possible, can extend transportation capabilities, making it easier to move goods and people across greater distances.

Finally, rebuilding transportation networks isn't only about physical infrastructure—it's also about reestablishing the social and logistical systems that keep a community functioning. This involves organizing work groups, coordinating the distribution of resources, and ensuring that everyone understands their role in maintaining and using the transportation system. Effective communication and cooperation are key to making these efforts successful. Regular community meetings or assemblies can be used to discuss transportation needs, address challenges, and plan for future repairs or improvements.

In conclusion, rebuilding transportation networks in a post-collapse world requires a combination of physical labor, innovative problem-solving, and community collaboration. By clearing and maintaining roads, adopting alternative methods of transportation, and creating an organized system for moving people and goods, communities can ensure they remain connected and resilient. These efforts support both immediate survival and long-term recovery, laying the foundation for a self-sustaining, adaptable community capable of thriving in a changed world.

6.3 Signaling for Help

In the wake of a disaster or collapse, one of the immediate concerns is the ability to signal for help, especially when cut off from conventional communication networks. Effective signaling can attract rescuers, alert nearby communities, or coordinate efforts within a group. The ability to create and use both visual and auditory signals is a crucial survival skill that can make the difference between being isolated and receiving timely assistance. Mastering these techniques requires an understanding of the environment, the available resources, and the context in which the signals will be used.

Visual signals are among the most effective ways to communicate over long distances, particularly when there is a clear line of sight. Signal fires are one of the oldest and most reliable methods for attracting attention. To create an effective signal fire, location is key—elevated areas such as hilltops or clearings offer the best visibility. The fire itself should be built large and hot to produce thick smoke that can be seen from far away. Using green vegetation, rubber, or oil can enhance the amount of smoke, making the signal more visible during the day. For nighttime signaling, keeping a stockpile of dry wood or other flammable materials ensures the fire burns brightly. Arranging the fires in patterns—such as three fires in a triangular formation or a straight line—can indicate distress, which is universally recognized as a call for help. It's also important to maintain the fire continuously until help arrives or other communication methods are established.

In addition to signal fires, other visual signaling methods include the use of mirrors, flares, and brightly colored fabrics or flags. Mirrors can reflect sunlight over vast distances, creating flashes of light that are visible to aircraft, ships, or distant observers. The technique involves angling the mirror to catch sunlight and directing the reflected beam towards the intended target. This method requires clear skies and direct sunlight but is highly effective during daylight hours. Flares are another potent signaling tool, often used in maritime settings but equally useful on land. They produce bright light and sometimes smoke, drawing attention from miles away. However, flares have a limited duration and should be used strategically, perhaps in conjunction with ongoing visual signals like fires or flags.

Flags or pieces of brightly colored fabric can serve as improvised signal devices when placed in open, visible areas or waved to attract attention. The international distress signal of waving a flag or any visible object overhead is a simple yet effective way to signal distress. In snow-covered or desert environments, using materials that contrast sharply with the surroundings increases the visibility of your signal. Additionally, arranging rocks, logs, or any available materials in large, distinct shapes such as "SOS" or an arrow pointing in a particular direction can communicate specific messages to rescuers from the air.

Auditory signals complement visual signals, particularly in environments where visibility is limited or during nighttime. Whistles, horns, or makeshift sound devices like banging on metal objects can carry over long distances, particularly in open spaces or across water. The international distress signal for sound is three short bursts followed by three long bursts, then three short bursts again, repeated at intervals. This pattern is recognized globally as a call for help. In scenarios where a whistle or horn is unavailable, human voice signals like shouting or yelling in a specific rhythm can also be used, though these are less effective over long distances or in noisy environments.

The use of signal devices should be paired with an understanding of the context in which they are deployed. For instance, signaling in a densely wooded area may require a combination of loud sounds to penetrate the forest canopy and bright light sources like flares or fires to pierce through the shadows. In mountainous regions, echoes and reflections can distort sound, so visual signals may take precedence. Additionally, when signaling from a vehicle or building, using reflective surfaces or flashing lights can attract attention more effectively than sound alone.

Maintaining signals consistently over time is crucial, particularly in rescue scenarios where the arrival of help might take hours or even days. Having a plan for replenishing signal materials—such as additional firewood for signal fires or spare batteries for electronic devices—ensures that the signals can be sustained. Communities should designate individuals or teams responsible for monitoring and maintaining the signals, ensuring that they are kept active until help arrives. Regular training and drills on signal use can prepare community members to respond quickly and efficiently in an emergency, reducing panic and increasing the likelihood of successful rescue.

In summary, signaling for help involves more than just knowing how to start a fire or blow a whistle; it requires strategic thinking, environmental awareness, and the ability to sustain efforts over time. By mastering both visual and auditory signaling techniques, communities can enhance their chances of being found and assisted in the event of an emergency. These skills are essential not only for individual survival but also for the broader safety and cohesion of the community as it navigates the challenges of a post-collapse environment.

6.4 Long-Distance Travel and Exploration

As communities stabilize in the aftermath of a disaster or collapse, the need for long-distance travel and exploration becomes increasingly important. Whether for the purpose of scouting new resources, establishing connections with other communities, or simply mapping out the surrounding terrain, the ability to travel efficiently and safely over long distances is a critical skill. However, without modern technology like GPS or vehicles, long-distance travel poses significant challenges, requiring careful planning, physical endurance, and a deep understanding of traditional navigation techniques.

The first step in preparing for long-distance travel is thorough planning. This involves not only selecting the destination but also considering the safest and most efficient route to get there. Factors such as terrain, weather conditions, and potential hazards must be taken into account. For example, traveling through dense forests or mountainous areas requires different preparations compared to journeys across open plains or deserts. In addition to mapping out the route, it's essential to identify potential rest stops, water sources, and safe shelters along the way. Understanding the natural environment is crucial—knowing where to find edible plants, water, and safe resting places can make the difference between a successful journey and a dangerous ordeal.

Without the aid of modern navigational tools, travelers must rely on traditional techniques such as the use of maps, compasses, and natural landmarks. Creating a simple map of the area, even if it's just a rough sketch, provides a visual reference that can help travelers stay oriented. Compasses, which point to magnetic north, are invaluable for maintaining a consistent direction, especially in environments where landmarks are scarce. However, it's also important to know how to navigate without a compass. Natural indicators like the position of the sun and stars, the growth patterns of moss on trees, and the flow of rivers can all serve as guides. For instance, in the Northern Hemisphere, the North Star (Polaris) is a reliable indicator of true north at night, while the sun's position in the sky can help determine cardinal directions during the day.

Building simple maps based on exploration and shared knowledge can help future expeditions and provide a foundation for understanding the larger environment. As travelers explore new areas, they can add details to these maps, such as noting the locations of water sources, fertile lands, and dangerous areas. Over time, these maps can evolve into more comprehensive documents that benefit the entire community, aiding in resource management, defense, and future expansion. Map-making also fosters a sense of collaboration, as different explorers contribute their findings, leading to a more nuanced understanding of the surrounding region.

Physical preparation is just as important as planning and navigation skills. Long-distance travel is physically demanding, particularly in rough or unfamiliar terrain. Travelers must be in good physical condition, capable of walking long distances while carrying supplies. Endurance training, such as regular hiking with a loaded backpack, can help build the necessary stamina. It's also important to pack wisely, carrying only essential items to avoid being weighed down. A well-prepared traveler's pack might include food, water, a first-aid kit, tools for making fire and shelter, and a basic navigation kit (such as a compass, map, and signaling devices). Lightweight, durable clothing that can protect against the elements is also crucial, as is sturdy footwear designed for the terrain.

Long-distance travel also involves psychological challenges. The isolation and uncertainty of traveling through unfamiliar territory can be daunting, particularly in a post-collapse world where dangers are ever-present. Mental resilience is key to overcoming these challenges. Travelers must be prepared to face setbacks, such as adverse weather, injuries, or unexpected obstacles, with calmness and adaptability. Having a clear purpose for the journey—whether it's to find a new water source, establish contact with another community, or explore potential agricultural land—helps maintain focus and motivation, even in difficult conditions.

Finally, successful long-distance travel requires a strong emphasis on safety and risk management. Traveling in groups is generally safer than traveling alone, as it provides mutual support and protection against threats. Groups can share the burden of carrying supplies, watch out for each other's well-being, and respond more effectively to emergencies. Establishing clear communication protocols, such as designated meeting points and signals for distress, further enhances safety. In the event that a traveler becomes separated from the group, having a prearranged plan for reuniting can prevent panic and ensure that the journey continues smoothly.

In conclusion, long-distance travel and exploration are vital for the expansion and sustainability of a post-collapse community. These endeavors require careful planning, physical and mental preparation, and a deep understanding of traditional navigation methods. By mastering these skills, communities can explore new territories, forge connections with other groups, and secure the resources necessary for long-term survival. As communities begin to rebuild and expand, the ability to navigate and explore the surrounding world will become increasingly important, laying the groundwork for a new era of discovery and growth.

Chapter 7: Power and Energy Solutions

Energy is the driving force behind progress and essential for rebuilding and maintaining a functioning community. In this chapter, you will learn how to tap into renewable energy sources and design sustainable power systems that can meet the ongoing needs of your community. These systems not only help reduce reliance on finite resources but also promote environmental stewardship and long-term resilience. By embracing renewable energy options such as solar, wind, hydro, and biomass, you can create a reliable and sustainable energy infrastructure that supports everything from basic needs like lighting and cooking to powering critical systems like healthcare and communication. This chapter will guide you through the process of harnessing these energy sources, enabling your community to thrive while minimizing environmental impact.

7.1. Harnessing Solar Energy

In the pursuit of rebuilding a self-sufficient society, harnessing solar energy stands out as one of the most practical, sustainable, and abundant solutions available. Solar energy offers a renewable source of power that can be used for a variety of essential tasks, from heating water to cooking food. As technology continues to improve, solar systems have become more accessible, even in a post-collapse world. By understanding how to build, maintain, and effectively use solar energy, communities can drastically reduce their reliance on finite resources and establish a more resilient and independent energy infrastructure.

One of the most efficient ways to harness solar energy is through the use of solar panels, which convert sunlight directly into electricity. While the process of building and maintaining solar panels might seem complex at first, it is entirely feasible with the right materials and knowledge. Solar panels are typically composed of photovoltaic (PV) cells, which convert sunlight into direct current (DC) electricity. Although creating PV cells from scratch requires advanced technology, repurposing solar panels from abandoned buildings or salvaging damaged ones can be a practical alternative. Repairing and reassembling these panels involves basic electrical concepts like wiring, soldering, and voltage regulation. Once the panels are repaired or assembled, they must be positioned at an optimal angle—usually around 30 degrees, facing south in the Northern Hemisphere—to ensure maximum exposure to sunlight throughout the day.

Alongside building the solar panels, it is essential to integrate them into a functioning electrical system. This involves setting up an inverter to convert the DC electricity produced by the solar panels into alternating current (AC), which is commonly used by most household appliances. Additionally, battery storage systems are crucial for storing any excess energy produced during sunny periods, which can be used during cloudy days or at night. Regular maintenance, such as cleaning the panels to remove dust and debris and checking electrical connections for wear, helps ensure the system runs efficiently. By mastering these skills, communities can create a reliable and sustainable electricity source that is independent of external power grids, ensuring long-term energy resilience.

Beyond electricity, solar energy can be harnessed for water heating, which is vital for both household and agricultural purposes. Solar water heaters use the sun's energy to directly heat water, offering an efficient solution to providing hot water without relying on electricity or fuel. There are several designs for solar water heaters, from basic batch systems where water is heated in an insulated tank exposed to the sun, to more advanced systems that circulate water through solar collectors before storing it in a separate insulated tank. Building a solar water heater involves materials like black-painted metal pipes, which absorb heat from the sun, and glass or clear plastic covers that trap the heat inside, creating a greenhouse effect. By understanding the principles of thermal mass and heat transfer, communities can design and construct solar water heaters that meet household or community needs, significantly reducing reliance on traditional water heating methods.

In addition to water heating, solar energy can also be used for cooking and food preservation. Solar cookers use reflective surfaces, such as aluminum foil or mirrors, to focus sunlight onto a cooking pot or surface, generating enough heat to prepare meals. Solar cookers can be constructed from simple, accessible materials like cardboard, glass, and reflective foil, making them ideal even in resource-scarce environments. These cookers are particularly beneficial in areas where fuel is either expensive or in short supply, as they eliminate the need for wood, gas, or electricity to cook food. Similarly, solar dehydrators utilize the sun's heat to dry fruits, vegetables, and meat, preserving them for long-term storage. A basic solar dehydrator can be built using a wooden frame, mesh trays for food, and a glass or plastic cover to trap heat. Proper ventilation is essential to ensure the moisture is efficiently removed from the food, preventing spoilage and ensuring effective preservation.

By adopting solar energy through these various applications, communities can significantly increase their energy independence and sustainability. Solar panels, water heaters, cookers, and dehydrators offer practical solutions for daily needs, helping communities reduce their reliance on external energy sources. The fact that the sun's energy is both free and abundant makes it one of the most reliable resources to harness, and by mastering the methods to effectively capture and utilize this energy, communities can take a significant step toward building a self-sufficient and sustainable society. In doing so, solar energy not only addresses immediate needs but also strengthens long-term community resilience, providing an essential foundation for rebuilding in a world that requires innovative, resourceful solutions.

7.2 Wind and Water Power

While solar energy is a versatile and widely applicable solution, it is not always reliable, especially in regions with limited sunlight. In such cases, harnessing the power of wind and water can provide essential energy alternatives. Wind and water power have been used for centuries to perform tasks such as grinding grain, pumping water, and generating electricity. By constructing and utilizing wind turbines and water wheels, communities can tap into these natural forces to generate power, ensuring a more diverse and stable energy supply. Integrating wind and water energy into the community's energy grid can enhance resilience and sustainability, especially when combined with solar power.

Wind turbines are one of the most effective ways to generate electricity from wind. A wind turbine works by converting the kinetic energy of the wind into mechanical energy, which is then converted into electrical energy through a generator. Building a wind turbine requires a few key components: blades, a rotor, a generator, and a tower. The blades, typically made from lightweight materials such as wood, fiberglass, or metal, capture the wind's energy and cause the rotor to spin. This spinning motion drives the generator, which produces electricity. The tower, which raises the turbine high above the ground, is crucial for accessing stronger and more consistent winds, as wind speeds generally increase with altitude.

Constructing a wind turbine from scratch can be challenging, especially without access to advanced tools and materials. However, repurposing materials from abandoned structures or scavenging parts from existing wind turbines can make the process more feasible. Maintenance is also a key consideration; regular inspections of the blades, bearings, and electrical connections are necessary to ensure the turbine operates efficiently. In regions where wind is a consistent and strong natural resource, wind turbines can provide a reliable source of electricity, particularly when combined with battery storage systems to capture energy for use during periods of calm.

In addition to wind power, water power offers another reliable energy source, particularly in areas with flowing rivers or streams. Water wheels and micro-hydro systems are effective ways to harness the energy of moving water. A water wheel, one of the oldest forms of mechanical energy conversion, uses the force of flowing water to turn a wheel, which can then power a mill, pump, or generator. Water wheels can be constructed from wood, metal, or a combination of both, depending on the resources available. The key to an effective water wheel is proper placement in a fast-moving section of a river or stream, where the flow of water can generate sufficient force to turn the wheel. This mechanical energy can be used directly for tasks such as grinding grain or can be converted into electricity with the addition of a generator.

Micro-hydro systems, on the other hand, are more sophisticated and are designed specifically for generating electricity. These systems divert a portion of a river or stream through a pipeline to a turbine, which spins a generator to produce electricity. Micro-hydro systems are particularly efficient because water, unlike wind or solar energy, provides a consistent and predictable power source, as long as the water flow is maintained. Constructing a micro-hydro system requires careful planning and understanding of the local water flow, as well as access to materials such as pipes, turbines, and generators. However, once established, these systems can provide a reliable and continuous supply of electricity with minimal maintenance.

Integrating wind and water energy into a community's energy grid involves more than just building the necessary infrastructure; it also requires coordination and management to ensure that the energy generated is used efficiently. Communities must establish protocols for distributing power, maintaining equipment, and balancing the load between different energy sources. For example, during periods of low wind, the community might rely more heavily on water or solar power, while during periods of drought, wind and solar might take precedence. Effective energy management ensures that all available resources are used to their fullest potential, reducing waste and maximizing the community's energy security.

In conclusion, wind and water power are invaluable resources for any community seeking to build a resilient and sustainable energy infrastructure. By mastering the construction and maintenance of wind turbines, water wheels, and micro-hydro systems, communities can diversify their energy sources and reduce their dependence on any single power source. This not only enhances the stability of their energy supply but also prepares them for a wide range of environmental conditions and challenges, ensuring that they can thrive even in the most difficult circumstances.

7.3 Bioenergy and Sustainable Fuels

In a post-collapse world, where traditional energy sources may become scarce or entirely unavailable, the ability to produce energy from organic materials is a crucial survival skill. Bioenergy, derived from biomass such as wood, agricultural waste, and organic matter, provides a renewable and sustainable source of fuel that can power homes, cook food, and even generate electricity. The key to leveraging bioenergy effectively lies in understanding how to convert raw organic materials into usable energy forms, such as biofuels, biogas, and charcoal. These methods not only reduce reliance on diminishing fossil fuel reserves but also help communities manage waste more sustainably by turning it into valuable resources.

One of the most practical applications of bioenergy is the production of biofuels, which can be created from a variety of organic materials, including crops, animal fats, and even algae. Biofuels, such as ethanol and biodiesel, can be produced through relatively simple processes that can be scaled according to the community's needs. For instance, ethanol can be made by fermenting sugar-rich crops like corn, sugarcane, or fruit waste. The fermentation process involves converting the sugars in these materials into alcohol using yeast, which can then be distilled to increase its purity. The resulting ethanol can be used as a fuel for modified engines, cooking stoves, or even as a disinfectant. Biodiesel, on the other hand, is produced by chemically reacting vegetable oils or animal fats with an alcohol like methanol in a process known as transesterification. The biodiesel produced can power diesel engines and generators, providing a sustainable alternative to traditional diesel fuel.

The production of biofuels requires not only the raw materials but also the appropriate equipment and knowledge. Distillation setups for ethanol can be constructed from basic materials like metal drums, copper tubing, and heat sources, while biodiesel production requires mixing tanks, separation units, and safety measures to handle the chemical reactions involved. Communities must also consider the sustainability of their feedstocks; using food crops for biofuel production might not be viable in a situation where food security is a concern. Therefore, focusing on non-food crops, agricultural waste, or even algae cultivation can provide a more sustainable feedstock for biofuel production. By mastering these processes, communities can create a local, renewable fuel supply that supports transportation, electricity generation, and cooking needs, reducing their dependence on external resources.

In addition to liquid biofuels, biogas is another valuable form of bioenergy that can be produced from organic waste materials. Biogas is primarily composed of methane and carbon dioxide, and it is generated through the anaerobic digestion of organic matter, such as animal manure, food waste, and plant material. This process occurs in a biogas digester, a sealed container where organic materials are broken down by bacteria in the absence of oxygen. The resulting biogas can be captured and used as a fuel for cooking, heating, or even generating electricity through a biogas generator. The digested material, known as digestate, is a nutrient-rich byproduct that can be used as a fertilizer, closing the loop in the community's waste management and agricultural processes.

Constructing a biogas digester can be done with locally available materials, such as large plastic or metal drums, pipes, and valves for gas collection. The digester must be airtight to ensure the anaerobic process, and it should be located in a warm area to maintain the activity of the bacteria. Regular feeding of the digester with organic waste and periodic stirring ensures efficient gas production. Communities can scale their biogas production to meet their energy needs, from small household digesters to larger community-scale systems. Biogas is especially valuable in areas where wood or other traditional fuels are scarce, providing a renewable and clean-burning alternative that can reduce deforestation and indoor air pollution.

Moreover, sustainable stoves and ovens designed to use biofuels or biogas can further enhance the efficiency of these energy sources. Traditional open fires, often used for cooking in resource-limited settings, are inefficient and produce harmful smoke that can lead to respiratory problems. In contrast, fuel-efficient stoves and ovens are designed to burn biofuels more completely, using less fuel and producing less smoke. Rocket stoves, for example, are highly efficient wood-burning stoves that use a small combustion chamber to create a hot, focused flame with minimal fuel. These stoves can be built using simple materials like bricks, metal cans, and insulation, making them accessible to communities with limited resources. Similarly, biogas stoves are designed to burn methane cleanly and efficiently, providing a safe and convenient way to cook food.

The integration of bioenergy into a community's energy mix not only provides a sustainable alternative to fossil fuels but also enhances resilience by utilizing local resources and reducing waste. By producing biofuels, biogas, and fuel-efficient stoves, communities can create a closed-loop system that supports their energy needs while promoting environmental sustainability. These technologies empower communities to become more self-sufficient, reducing their vulnerability to external energy disruptions and contributing to a more sustainable way of living.

7.4 Energy Storage Solutions

While generating renewable energy is essential for a self-sufficient community, the ability to store that energy for later use is equally important. Energy storage systems are crucial for managing the intermittent nature of renewable energy sources like solar and wind, which do not always produce power when it is needed. Effective energy storage solutions ensure that the energy generated during periods of abundance—such as sunny or windy days—can be saved and used during periods of scarcity, such as at night or on calm days. Understanding how to design, build, and maintain these storage systems is key to creating a reliable and resilient energy infrastructure.

Battery storage systems are among the most common and versatile methods for storing electrical energy. Batteries store energy in chemical form and release it as electricity when needed. There are several types of batteries that can be used for energy storage, including lead-acid, lithium-ion, and nickel-cadmium batteries, each with its advantages and drawbacks. Lead-acid batteries, for instance, are widely used in off-grid systems due to their reliability and relatively low cost, though they are heavy and have a limited lifespan. Lithium-ion batteries are more expensive but offer higher energy density, longer life, and greater efficiency. Nickel-cadmium batteries are durable and can operate in a wide range of temperatures but are less environmentally friendly due to the toxic materials they contain.

Designing a battery storage system involves determining the community's energy needs, selecting the appropriate type of battery, and configuring the system to store and deliver power efficiently. This includes sizing the battery bank to match the energy production and consumption patterns, ensuring proper ventilation to prevent overheating, and integrating charge controllers to protect the batteries from overcharging or deep discharge. It is also important to consider the safety aspects of battery storage, such as preventing short circuits, ensuring proper grounding, and regularly inspecting the batteries for signs of wear or damage.

Beyond electrical storage, thermal mass storage is another effective method for managing energy, particularly for heating and cooling applications. Thermal mass refers to materials that can absorb, store, and release heat energy over time. Common materials used for thermal mass storage include water, concrete, stone, and brick. These materials can be incorporated into building designs to regulate indoor temperatures, reducing the need for active heating and cooling systems. For example, a concrete floor or wall can absorb heat during the day and release it slowly at night, maintaining a more stable indoor temperature. This passive heating and cooling technique is especially valuable in climates with significant temperature fluctuations between day and night.

Thermal mass storage can also be used in conjunction with solar energy systems. For instance, solar water heaters can store thermal energy in water tanks, providing hot water even when the sun is not shining. Similarly, solar thermal panels can heat a thermal mass, such as a large masonry structure, which then radiates heat into a building during cooler periods. These systems are low-tech, require minimal maintenance, and can significantly reduce a community's reliance on conventional energy sources for heating and cooling.

Maintaining and repairing energy storage systems is crucial for ensuring their long-term reliability and efficiency. Batteries, for example, require regular maintenance, such as checking the electrolyte levels in lead-acid batteries, cleaning terminals, and equalizing charge levels to prevent sulfation. Lithium-ion batteries, while lower maintenance, need to be monitored for overheating and voltage imbalances. For thermal mass systems, maintenance might involve inspecting insulation, sealing cracks in masonry, or ensuring that heat transfer systems are functioning properly. Communities should train members in the basics of energy storage maintenance and repair, empowering them to troubleshoot issues and extend the lifespan of these critical systems.

Furthermore, the integration of energy storage systems into the broader community energy grid requires careful planning and management. Balancing the load between generation, storage, and consumption is essential to avoid overloading systems or running out of stored energy during critical times. Smart inverters and energy management systems can help automate this process, ensuring that energy is used efficiently and that storage systems are charged and discharged at optimal times. In a resource-constrained environment, such management is crucial for maximizing the utility of every watt of power generated and stored.

In conclusion, energy storage solutions are a cornerstone of a resilient and sustainable energy infrastructure. By mastering the design, construction, and maintenance of battery storage systems, thermal mass storage, and other energy storage technologies, communities can ensure a stable and reliable energy supply, even when renewable energy sources are intermittent. These systems not only enhance the efficiency and reliability of the community's energy grid but also provide a critical buffer against energy shortages, ensuring that the community can thrive even in the most challenging conditions.

7.5 Energy Conservation Strategies

While generating and storing energy is crucial for any self-sufficient community, equally important is the efficient use of that energy. Energy conservation strategies are essential for minimizing waste, reducing the overall demand on energy systems, and ensuring that available resources are used as effectively as possible. By focusing on energy conservation, communities can stretch their energy supplies further, reduce the frequency of power shortages, and enhance their overall sustainability. These strategies not only help in managing scarce resources but also contribute to a more comfortable and resilient living environment.

One of the most effective ways to conserve energy is through proper insulation of homes and communal buildings. Insulation plays a critical role in maintaining indoor temperatures, reducing the need for heating in the winter and cooling in the summer. Well-insulated buildings retain heat during cold periods and keep the interior cool during hot weather, thus reducing the reliance on active heating and cooling systems, which are often energy-intensive. There are various materials that can be used for insulation, depending on availability and the specific needs of the building. Common insulation materials include fiberglass, cellulose, foam, and natural materials like straw, wool, or recycled textiles. In a post-collapse scenario, communities may need to get creative with insulation materials, using whatever is readily available, such as old clothing, newspapers, or even earth.

The key areas to insulate include walls, roofs, floors, and windows. Double-glazing windows or using heavy curtains can significantly reduce heat loss, while insulating the attic or roof space prevents warm air from escaping upwards. Draft-proofing doors and windows is another simple yet effective measure; even small gaps can lead to significant energy loss. Sealing these gaps with weatherstripping or caulking ensures that the warm air stays inside during winter and that cool air is preserved during summer. In addition to these measures, designing buildings with energy efficiency in mind, such as incorporating passive solar design, can also reduce the energy needed to maintain comfortable temperatures. For example, placing windows on the south side of a building in the Northern Hemisphere maximizes solar gain in the winter, while overhangs or shading devices can reduce heat during the summer.

Beyond structural improvements, energy-efficient cooking and heating systems are critical for conserving energy in daily life. Traditional open fires and inefficient stoves consume large amounts of fuel, much of which is wasted in the form of heat loss. By contrast, fuel-efficient stoves, such as rocket stoves, are designed to burn fuel more completely and direct more of the heat to the cooking surface or into the living space. Rocket stoves achieve this by using an insulated combustion chamber that ensures a hotter and more efficient burn, requiring less fuel to achieve the same cooking or heating results. These stoves can be constructed from simple materials like bricks, metal cans, or clay, making them accessible even in resource-scarce environments. Similarly, solar cookers and ovens, which use reflective surfaces to concentrate sunlight for cooking, provide an energy-free alternative to traditional cooking methods, particularly in sunny climates.

For heating, the use of thermal mass and efficient wood stoves can significantly reduce the amount of fuel needed. Thermal mass, as discussed earlier, involves using materials that absorb and slowly release heat, such as stone, concrete, or water. Incorporating thermal mass into a building's design helps maintain a stable indoor temperature, reducing the need for additional heating. For example, a masonry heater, which is a type of wood stove built with a large thermal mass, can store heat from a single, efficient fire and radiate it for hours, providing consistent warmth with minimal fuel use. These systems are particularly effective in cold climates, where the need for heating is constant and fuel resources may be limited.

Another critical aspect of energy conservation is community energy management and rationing. In a post-collapse environment, energy resources are likely to be limited, making it necessary to prioritize their use. Establishing a system of energy rationing ensures that all members of the community have access to the energy they need while preventing overuse and waste. This might involve setting limits on the amount of electricity or fuel each household can use, scheduling times for communal cooking or heating, or rotating the use of high-energy appliances like generators or pumps. Rationing can be managed through simple systems like token distribution, where each household receives a certain number of energy tokens that can be exchanged for fuel, electricity, or access to communal energy resources.

Community energy management also involves educating members about energy conservation practices and encouraging behavioral changes that reduce energy consumption. This can include turning off lights and appliances when not in use, using energy-efficient cooking methods, sharing rides to reduce fuel consumption, and optimizing the use of natural light and ventilation to reduce the need for artificial lighting and cooling. Regular community meetings can be used to discuss energy usage, share tips and techniques for conserving energy, and address any issues or concerns related to energy rationing. By fostering a culture of energy awareness and cooperation, communities can ensure that their energy resources are used wisely and sustainably.

Finally, it is important to consider the long-term sustainability of energy conservation strategies. As communities grow and evolve, their energy needs will change, and so too must their conservation strategies. Continuous monitoring of energy usage, regular maintenance of energy systems, and ongoing education about energy conservation are all necessary to maintain efficiency and adapt to new challenges. By making energy conservation a core part of their survival strategy, communities can build a resilient and sustainable energy infrastructure that supports their long-term survival and prosperity.

In conclusion, energy conservation strategies are essential for any community striving for self-sufficiency and sustainability. By insulating buildings, using energy-efficient cooking and heating systems, and implementing community-wide energy management practices, communities can significantly reduce their energy consumption and extend the life of their energy resources. These strategies not only make the most of the energy that is available but also help create a more resilient and sustainable living environment, ensuring that the community can thrive even in the face of limited resources and challenging conditions.

Chapter 8: Creating Adaptive Governance and Resilient Societies

Effective leadership and fair governance are crucial pillars for maintaining social cohesion in any society, particularly in the aftermath of a collapse. Strong leadership not only guides a community through challenges but also fosters a sense of unity and shared purpose. In this chapter, we will explore how to establish and nurture effective leadership, create just and equitable laws, and cultivate a culture that prioritizes cooperation, justice, and resilience. Building such a framework ensures that a community is not only able to survive but also thrive in the face of adversity, supporting the development of a thriving, sustainable society rooted in trust and mutual respect.

8.1 Establishing Leadership

In the aftermath of a societal collapse, establishing effective leadership becomes one of the most critical and urgent steps in rebuilding a functional and resilient community. Without strong and reliable leadership, efforts to organize, protect, and sustain the group can quickly deteriorate into chaos, confusion, and division. Leadership, in this context, is not about asserting power or control for its own sake; rather, it is about guiding the community through difficult decisions, coordinating resources, and fostering a collective sense of unity and purpose. In order to achieve this, it is essential to identify natural leaders within the community, establish a governance structure that encourages participation, and develop decision-making processes that are transparent, inclusive, and reflective of the needs of the entire group.

Identifying natural leaders within a community begins with recognizing individuals who embody the qualities necessary to inspire trust and cooperation among their peers. These qualities include integrity, empathy, problem-solving abilities, and the capacity to remain calm and focused under pressure. In times of crisis, natural leaders often emerge—those who willingly take responsibility, offer solutions, and bring people together. These individuals are likely to be the most effective in leadership roles, as their actions resonate with the needs of the community. However, it is important to avoid consolidating power in the hands of a single leader. Instead, a leadership team or council should be formed to distribute responsibilities and ensure that a variety of perspectives are included in decision-making processes.

Creating a governance body, such as a council, is a crucial step in formalizing leadership within the community. This council should consist of individuals who represent different segments of the population, ensuring that the diverse needs and concerns of the community are addressed. For instance, the council might include leaders from various family groups, skilled tradespeople, healthcare providers, and those in charge of security and resource management. The primary function of the council is to make decisions that benefit the entire community, allocate resources, and resolve conflicts. To operate effectively, the council must be transparent, regularly communicating its decisions and the rationale behind them to the wider community.

The decision-making process within the council must be designed to encourage broad participation from all members of the community, not just from the council itself. This can be achieved by holding regular meetings where community members are invited to voice their opinions, propose solutions, and vote on important issues. Such participatory decision-making fosters a sense of ownership and shared responsibility, which is essential for maintaining social cohesion and trust. Moreover, it ensures that decisions are made with input from those who will be directly impacted by them, leading to more sustainable, effective, and widely supported outcomes.

To avoid the dangers of centralized power, the council should implement mechanisms for accountability. This includes setting term limits for council members, allowing for regular elections or rotations in leadership roles, and establishing systems for removing or replacing leaders who fail to fulfill their duties. By ensuring that leadership remains dynamic and responsive to the community's needs, these mechanisms help prevent the abuse of power and preserve the legitimacy of the governance structure. The ability to hold leaders accountable strengthens the trust the community places in their governance system and ensures it continues to serve the best interests of all.

In conclusion, establishing strong and effective leadership in a post-collapse community involves identifying natural leaders, creating a governance structure that represents all parts of the population, and developing decision-making processes that are inclusive, transparent, and accountable. By fostering a leadership structure that encourages participation, collaboration, and responsiveness, the community can build a solid foundation for effective governance, which will contribute to its long-term resilience and sustainability. This approach to leadership ensures that the community remains united, adaptive, and capable of meeting the challenges of rebuilding a stable and thriving society.

8.2 Creating Laws and Regulations

Once a leadership structure is in place, the next critical step in rebuilding governance is the establishment of laws and regulations that provide a framework for maintaining order, ensuring fairness, and promoting the well-being of the community. In a world where established legal systems may no longer function, communities must create their own code of conduct tailored to their unique circumstances and values. This process involves not only drafting and enforcing rules but also adapting them as the community evolves and grows. Additionally, setting up mechanisms for conflict resolution, addressing grievances, and rehabilitating offenders is essential for maintaining peace and justice within the community.

The first task in creating laws and regulations is to establish a code of conduct that outlines the basic principles and rules that all community members are expected to follow. This code should reflect the core values of the community, such as respect for others, cooperation, honesty, and the protection of shared resources. The process of drafting this code should be collaborative, with input from a wide range of community members to ensure that the rules are fair, relevant, and widely accepted. The code of conduct should address key areas such as property rights, resource allocation, interpersonal behavior, and the consequences for violating the rules.

Once the code of conduct is established, the community must develop a system for enforcing these rules fairly and consistently. This requires the establishment of a group or individual responsible for monitoring compliance and addressing violations. In many cases, this role may be fulfilled by a designated council member or a small team tasked with upholding the community's laws. It is crucial that enforcement is carried out impartially, without favoritism or bias, to maintain the integrity of the legal system and the trust of the community.

As the community grows and evolves, it will be necessary to adapt and expand the laws to address new challenges and circumstances. This may include creating more detailed regulations around resource management, trade, and interactions with other communities. The process of adapting laws should be flexible and responsive to the changing needs of the community, with regular reviews and opportunities for community members to propose changes or new regulations. By keeping the legal framework dynamic, the community can ensure that its laws remain relevant and effective.

In addition to establishing rules and enforcing them, it is important to set up a system for resolving disputes and addressing grievances within the community. This can be achieved by creating a community court or mediation system where conflicts can be aired and resolved in a fair and transparent manner. The court or mediation body should be composed of respected community members who are seen as impartial and capable of making balanced judgments. Their role is to listen to both sides of a dispute, consider the evidence, and provide a resolution that is in line with the community's laws and values. By providing a structured process for conflict resolution, the community can prevent disputes from escalating into violence or division.

Addressing grievances is not just about resolving disputes but also about maintaining social harmony and ensuring that all community members feel heard and respected. This includes providing avenues for individuals to express their concerns and frustrations, whether through formal channels like the community court or more informal settings like community meetings. By addressing grievances promptly and fairly, the community can prevent small issues from growing into larger problems that could threaten the social fabric.

Finally, a critical aspect of maintaining peace and justice within the community is the rehabilitation and reintegration of offenders. In a small, close-knit community, the goal should not only be to punish wrongdoers but also to help them reintegrate into the community as productive members. This might involve restorative justice practices, where offenders are required to make amends to those they have harmed, as well as providing opportunities for education, skill-building, or other forms of support that can help them avoid future offenses. By focusing on rehabilitation rather than retribution, the community can strengthen social bonds and reduce the likelihood of recurring conflicts.

In conclusion, creating laws and regulations in a post-collapse community involves establishing a code of conduct, enforcing rules fairly, adapting laws as needed, and setting up systems for conflict resolution and rehabilitation. These legal frameworks are essential for maintaining order, ensuring fairness, and fostering a sense of justice and community cohesion. By building a legal system that is flexible, fair, and focused on the well-being of all members, the community can create a stable and just society that is capable of withstanding the challenges of a post-collapse world.

8.3 Building a Resilient Culture

Building a resilient culture is the cornerstone of any successful community, particularly in a post-collapse world where traditional societal structures have broken down. Culture serves as the glue that binds a community together, offering a shared identity, values, and sense of purpose that guide collective actions. In the absence of the old societal norms, the task of creating a new culture becomes not just important but essential for the survival and thriving of the group. This culture must be rooted in principles that promote cooperation, adaptability, and sustainability, while also honoring and preserving the unique achievements and traditions that emerge within the community.

One of the first steps in cultivating a resilient culture is to actively celebrate the community's achievements and milestones. In a world where the daily struggle for survival can easily overshadow moments of progress, it is crucial to create space for recognition and celebration. These moments of acknowledgment help reinforce the community's collective spirit, providing psychological and emotional sustenance that can fortify the group against the hardships they face. Whether it is the successful completion of a harvest, the construction of a new shelter, or the birth of a child, celebrating these events reinforces the community's shared goals and the value of every member's contributions. These celebrations also serve to cement memories that can be passed down through stories and rituals, becoming a part of the community's evolving narrative.

Traditions play a pivotal role in the formation and preservation of culture. In the wake of a collapse, some pre-existing traditions may no longer be relevant or feasible, while new ones will need to be created to suit the community's current reality. The creation of new traditions should be an organic process, one that arises naturally from the community's experiences, values, and needs. For example, the community might establish a yearly festival to mark the start of the growing season, or a communal meal to celebrate the end of the harvest. These traditions, while simple, help to instill a sense of normalcy and continuity, offering a rhythm to life that contrasts with the uncertainties of the outside world. Over time, these traditions become part of the community's identity, providing comfort and a sense of belonging to its members.

A resilient culture must also promote the values of cooperation and mutual aid. In a survival scenario, individualism can be detrimental to the well-being of the group. Instead, the culture should emphasize the importance of working together, sharing resources, and supporting one another. This can be encouraged through community activities that require collective effort, such as building projects, communal gardening, or group hunting expeditions. These activities not only provide essential resources but also foster strong interpersonal bonds and a sense of collective responsibility. By embedding the value of cooperation into the daily life of the community, these practices become second nature, reducing conflicts and ensuring that the group can operate as a cohesive unit in the face of challenges.

Sustainability is another core principle that must be integrated into the community's culture. In a post-collapse world, the careless exploitation of resources can lead to disaster. A sustainable culture recognizes the finite nature of these resources and prioritizes their careful management and renewal. This involves teaching community members to live within their means, minimize waste, and use resources in a way that preserves them for future generations. For example, agricultural practices should emphasize crop rotation, composting, and the use of natural fertilizers to maintain soil health. Similarly, the community should prioritize the use of renewable energy sources, such as solar or wind power, and develop technologies that minimize environmental impact. By making sustainability a cultural norm, the community ensures its long-term viability and reduces its vulnerability to external shocks.

Art, music, and literature play a critical role in reflecting and shaping the community's culture. In the absence of formal institutions, these creative expressions become the primary means of preserving the community's experiences, values, and aspirations. Encouraging the creation of art that reflects the community's struggles and triumphs not only provides a therapeutic outlet for individuals but also helps to build a collective identity. Songs that tell the stories of the community's history, paintings that depict significant events, and literature that explores the community's values all contribute to a rich cultural tapestry. These creative works can be passed down through generations, ensuring that the community's cultural heritage is preserved even as it continues to evolve.

Moreover, a resilient culture must be flexible and adaptable, capable of evolving in response to changing circumstances. This adaptability is crucial in a post-collapse environment, where the challenges and threats faced by the community can shift rapidly. A rigid culture that cannot accommodate change risks becoming obsolete or even harmful. Instead, the community should cultivate a culture that values innovation, experimentation, and learning. This might involve regular community discussions about what is working and what is not, encouraging members to propose new ideas and solutions, and being willing to adjust or abandon practices that no longer serve the community's best interests. By fostering a culture of continuous learning and adaptation, the community not only survives but thrives in an unpredictable world.

In conclusion, building a resilient culture is about more than just preserving traditions or celebrating achievements—it is about creating a living, breathing framework that supports the community's survival and growth. By emphasizing cooperation, sustainability, and adaptability, and by encouraging creative expression, the community can forge a strong cultural identity that unites its members and prepares them to face the future together. This culture will serve as the foundation upon which all other aspects of the community—its governance, economy, and social structures—are built, ensuring that the group remains resilient and cohesive in the face of whatever challenges lie ahead.

Chapter 9: Health and Medicine in a New World

Health is the cornerstone of any thriving community, and its importance becomes even more pronounced in a world where resources are scarce and systems have collapsed. In this chapter, we will explore how to build a resilient community health system, blending the wisdom of traditional medicine with the advancements of modern healthcare practices. We will also discuss strategies for preparing for medical emergencies, ensuring that the community has the necessary tools, knowledge, and resources to respond effectively in times of crisis. With a strong foundation in both preventative care and emergency medical preparedness, communities can not only survive but thrive, maintaining their health and well-being even when faced with limited resources. This chapter will guide you through the process of creating a sustainable health system that addresses the diverse needs of the community while maximizing available resources.

9.1 Building a Community Health System

In a post-collapse world, where modern healthcare infrastructure may be severely compromised or entirely absent, establishing a robust community health system becomes a critical and urgent priority. Without the resources provided by hospitals, pharmacies, and trained medical professionals, communities must assume responsibility for their own health needs. This involves identifying individuals within the community who can be trained as healthcare providers, setting up a basic health facility, and ensuring a reliable supply of essential medical resources. By building a health system from the ground up, communities can significantly improve their resilience, reduce mortality rates, and enhance the overall quality of life for their members.

The first step in creating a community health system is identifying individuals within the community who either possess or can acquire the necessary healthcare skills. Some people may already have medical training, such as former nurses, doctors, or paramedics, but it is equally important to recognize those who are willing and able to learn. Community-based training programs should be established to teach basic medical skills, such as wound care, administering first aid, and recognizing common illnesses. These programs can be led by experienced healthcare providers or guided by instructional manuals and resources that can be scavenged or created. The goal is to build a network of community health workers who can deliver care, offer guidance on health issues, and educate others on preventive health practices.

Once healthcare providers are identified and trained, the next step is to set up a community clinic or health post. While this facility doesn't need to be complex, it should be equipped to handle essential medical needs such as treating minor injuries, managing chronic conditions, and addressing common illnesses. The clinic should be centrally located for easy access by all community members and should include areas for patient consultation, treatment, and the safe storage of medical supplies. Basic medical equipment such as examination tables, sterilization tools, and essential medical instruments should be prioritized, alongside creating a clean, sanitary environment to prevent infections. If possible, the clinic should also have a dedicated space for quarantine to manage potential outbreaks of infectious diseases.

An integral aspect of the community health system is ensuring a steady and reliable medical supply chain. Since the ability to easily purchase or produce medical supplies may be limited, communities must devise creative ways to obtain, store, and distribute essential items like bandages, antiseptics, medications, and surgical tools. This may involve scavenging abandoned pharmacies and medical facilities, trading with neighboring communities, or learning to manufacture basic supplies locally. For instance, bandages can be made from clean cloth, while alcohol or iodine can be used to create basic antiseptics. A central storage area for these supplies, with careful inventory management, ensures that the community can respond effectively to medical needs as they arise. The supply chain should also include a strategy for securing and storing critical medications, especially those with long shelf lives or that are difficult to obtain.

In addition to physical medical supplies, a sustainable community health system must emphasize knowledge and education. This includes training healthcare providers in both modern and traditional medical practices, as well as educating the broader community about health, hygiene, and disease prevention. Regular workshops, training sessions, and informational talks can help spread vital health knowledge and ensure that everyone in the community is equipped to maintain their health and prevent the spread of diseases. By fostering a culture of health awareness, communities can reduce the burden on the healthcare system, improve overall well-being, and encourage self-sufficiency in managing their health.

By taking these comprehensive steps, communities can build a resilient health system that not only addresses immediate medical needs but also ensures long-term health sustainability and security.

9.2 Traditional and Herbal Medicine

In a world where access to modern medicine may be limited or nonexistent, traditional and herbal medicine becomes an invaluable resource for maintaining health and treating illness. Long before the advent of pharmaceuticals, people relied on the healing properties of plants and other natural substances to treat a wide range of ailments. Reviving this knowledge and integrating it with modern medical practices can provide communities with a powerful toolset for addressing health challenges in a post-collapse environment. By identifying and using medicinal plants, preparing and storing herbal remedies, and blending traditional practices with modern medicine, communities can enhance their self-reliance and improve their ability to care for the sick and injured.

The first step in harnessing the power of traditional and herbal medicine is to identify the medicinal plants that grow in the local environment. This requires a deep understanding of the local flora, as well as knowledge of which plants have therapeutic properties. In many regions, this knowledge may still exist within older generations or among those who practiced herbal medicine before the collapse. These individuals can be invaluable resources for teaching others about plant identification, harvesting techniques, and the preparation of remedies. Communities should make efforts to document this knowledge, creating written records or instructional guides that can be passed down and preserved for future generations.

Once the appropriate plants have been identified, the next step is to learn how to properly prepare and store herbal remedies. Different plants require different methods of preparation to unlock their medicinal properties. Some may need to be dried and ground into powders, while others are best used fresh in teas, poultices, or tinctures. It is important to learn these techniques to ensure that the remedies are both effective and safe. Drying herbs is one of the most common methods of preservation, as it allows the plant material to be stored for long periods without losing its potency. Herbs can be dried by hanging them in a well-ventilated area out of direct sunlight or by using solar dehydrators. Once dried, the herbs should be stored in airtight containers in a cool, dark place to maintain their effectiveness.

Tinctures, which are concentrated liquid extracts made by soaking herbs in alcohol or vinegar, are another popular form of herbal remedy. These can be particularly useful because they have a long shelf life and are easy to administer. Learning to make tinctures involves understanding the correct ratios of plant material to solvent and the appropriate soaking times to extract the active compounds. Similarly, salves and ointments can be made by infusing herbs into oils or fats, which can then be applied topically to treat wounds, rashes, and other skin conditions. By mastering these preparation techniques, communities can create a versatile herbal medicine cabinet capable of addressing a wide range of health issues.

Integrating traditional practices with modern medicine is another key aspect of creating a holistic community health system. While modern medicine excels in areas such as emergency care and surgery, traditional medicine offers valuable approaches to chronic conditions, preventive care, and overall wellness. For example, while antibiotics might be used to treat a severe infection, herbal remedies could be employed to support the immune system and aid in recovery. In cases where modern medications are unavailable, traditional remedies may provide an effective alternative. However, it is crucial to approach this integration with a careful, evidence-based mindset. Not all traditional practices are beneficial, and some may be harmful if used improperly. Therefore, communities should prioritize ongoing education and research, drawing from both scientific and traditional knowledge to determine the most effective treatments.

Moreover, the use of traditional and herbal medicine fosters a sense of connection to the natural world, which can be particularly important in a post-collapse environment. This connection reinforces the idea that the community is part of a larger ecosystem and that by caring for the environment, they are also caring for their own health. Encouraging sustainable harvesting practices, protecting local habitats, and cultivating medicinal plants in community gardens are all ways to ensure that these resources remain available for future generations. By embedding traditional and herbal medicine into the fabric of the community's health system, the group not only gains practical tools for survival but also strengthens its cultural and environmental ties.

In summary, traditional and herbal medicine offers a valuable complement to modern healthcare practices, particularly in a world where access to conventional medicine is limited. By identifying medicinal plants, mastering preparation and storage techniques, and integrating these practices with modern medicine, communities can build a more resilient and self-sufficient health system. This approach not only enhances the community's ability to care for its members but also fosters a deeper connection to the natural world and the cultural traditions that sustain it.

9.3 Preventive Healthcare and Hygiene

In a post-collapse world, where medical resources are scarce and professional healthcare may be limited, preventive healthcare and hygiene become the front lines in the battle against disease and illness. Without the luxury of modern medical infrastructure, the emphasis must shift from treating illnesses after they occur to preventing them from happening in the first place. This proactive approach is not only more sustainable but also crucial for the survival of the community. By understanding the importance of cleanliness, adopting effective sanitation practices, and promoting a culture of health, communities can significantly reduce the burden of disease and improve the overall quality of life.

The foundation of preventive healthcare in any community is cleanliness and sanitation. Clean living environments are essential to prevent the spread of infectious diseases, which can quickly decimate populations that lack access to adequate medical care. Proper waste management, regular cleaning of communal areas, and the maintenance of personal hygiene are critical components of this strategy. Communities must establish and enforce standards for waste disposal, ensuring that garbage is collected and processed in a way that does not attract pests or contaminate water sources. Composting toilets, greywater systems, and the careful management of organic waste can all contribute to maintaining a sanitary environment. Regular cleaning of living spaces, particularly areas where food is prepared and consumed, is also vital to prevent the buildup of harmful bacteria and other pathogens.

Hand hygiene is perhaps the most basic yet effective method for preventing the spread of disease. In the absence of modern plumbing, communities must find alternative ways to ensure that clean water and soap are available for handwashing. This might involve setting up communal handwashing stations equipped with simple foot-pump-operated water dispensers and soap. Educating community members, particularly children, about the importance of regular handwashing—especially after using the toilet, before eating, and after handling waste—is crucial. Additionally, making hand sanitizer using alcohol-based solutions can provide a backup when water is scarce. By ingraining these practices into daily routines, the community can create a culture of cleanliness that serves as a first line of defense against disease.

Sanitation practices extend beyond personal hygiene to include the safe preparation and storage of food and water. Contaminated food and water are common vectors for disease, and in a survival scenario, the community cannot afford widespread illness caused by preventable contamination. Proper cooking techniques, such as boiling water and thoroughly cooking meat, are essential for killing harmful pathogens. Food should be stored in secure, clean containers to prevent exposure to pests and bacteria. Additionally, communities should prioritize the construction of safe water collection and storage systems, such as rainwater harvesting setups with filtration systems, to ensure a reliable supply of clean drinking water. Regular inspection and maintenance of these systems are necessary to prevent contamination and ensure their continued effectiveness.

Vaccination, where possible, remains one of the most effective tools for preventing the spread of infectious diseases. While access to vaccines may be limited in a post-collapse world, any available vaccines should be prioritized and distributed to those most at risk, such as children, the elderly, and those with compromised immune systems. Communities should make efforts to acquire and store vaccines, possibly through barter or trade with other groups, and maintain cold storage facilities to preserve them. Education about the importance of vaccination and the diseases they prevent can help reduce hesitancy and ensure high uptake among community members. Where modern vaccines are unavailable, alternative strategies such as isolation of infected individuals, quarantine measures, and the promotion of herd immunity through natural exposure might need to be employed, though these come with significant risks.

Promoting healthy lifestyles and nutrition is another cornerstone of preventive healthcare. Proper nutrition is essential for maintaining a strong immune system, which in turn helps to fend off infections and diseases. In a post-collapse environment, where food sources may be limited, communities must focus on cultivating a balanced diet through sustainable agriculture. This includes growing a variety of crops that provide essential vitamins and minerals, raising livestock for protein, and foraging for wild edibles that can supplement the diet. Educating community members about the importance of a balanced diet and the nutritional value of locally available foods is key to ensuring that everyone has access to the nutrients they need to stay healthy.

Physical activity is also important for maintaining overall health. While daily survival tasks such as farming, hunting, and building provide some level of physical exertion, it is important to encourage additional forms of exercise that promote cardiovascular health, flexibility, and strength. Community activities, such as group walks, sports, or dance, can not only improve physical health but also strengthen social bonds and boost morale. Ensuring that all members of the community, regardless of age or physical ability, have opportunities to stay active contributes to a healthier, more resilient population.

Mental health is another critical aspect of preventive healthcare. The stresses of living in a post-collapse world, combined with the loss of loved ones and the daily struggle for survival, can take a significant toll on mental well-being. Communities must recognize the importance of mental health and provide support systems to help individuals cope with stress, anxiety, and trauma. This might involve setting up peer support groups, providing spaces for relaxation and reflection, and encouraging open communication about mental health issues. Activities that promote mental wellness, such as meditation, storytelling, and communal gatherings, can help build resilience and ensure that the community remains strong in the face of adversity.

In summary, preventive healthcare and hygiene are the bedrock of a resilient community in a post-collapse world. By prioritizing cleanliness, sanitation, vaccination, and healthy lifestyles, communities can prevent the spread of disease and maintain a high standard of health despite limited resources. These practices, when integrated into the daily life of the community, create a culture of health that not only enhances individual well-being but also strengthens the collective resilience of the group, ensuring its survival and prosperity in the long term.

9.4 Emergency Medical Response

In a world where access to professional medical care is limited or nonexistent, the ability to respond effectively to medical emergencies becomes a critical component of community survival. Whether dealing with injuries, sudden illnesses, or large-scale disease outbreaks, a well-prepared emergency medical response system can save lives and prevent minor issues from escalating into major crises. Establishing such a system requires training community members in essential medical skills, creating a network of first responders, and developing clear protocols for handling various types of medical emergencies. By building a robust emergency medical response infrastructure, communities can ensure that they are equipped to handle the inevitable health challenges that will arise in a post-collapse environment.

The foundation of any emergency medical response system is the training of individuals who can act as first responders. These first responders are the community's frontline defense against medical emergencies, capable of providing immediate care in the crucial minutes or hours before more advanced treatment can be administered. Training programs should focus on teaching basic first aid, CPR, wound management, and the stabilization of injuries such as fractures and sprains. These skills can be taught by more experienced healthcare providers within the community or through the use of manuals and instructional materials. It is important that training is not limited to a select few but is made accessible to as many community members as possible, ensuring that there is always someone nearby who can respond in an emergency.

Once a core group of first responders is trained, the next step is to organize them into a network that can be mobilized quickly when needed. This network should include individuals from various parts of the community, ensuring broad coverage and the ability to respond rapidly to emergencies wherever they occur. Communication systems, such as hand-held radios or signal systems, should be established to alert first responders to an emergency and coordinate their actions. It is also important to conduct regular drills and simulations to ensure that the response network is well-practiced and able to function effectively under pressure. These drills should cover a range of scenarios, from individual injuries to larger-scale incidents like fires, natural disasters, or disease outbreaks, allowing first responders to build the experience and confidence needed to act swiftly and decisively.

Developing protocols for handling different types of medical emergencies is another critical aspect of emergency medical response. These protocols provide a clear, step-by-step guide for first responders and other community members to follow, ensuring that everyone knows what to do in an emergency and that actions are coordinated and efficient. Protocols should cover the full spectrum of potential emergencies, from minor injuries to life-threatening situations. For example, a protocol for a serious injury might include steps such as assessing the scene for safety, controlling bleeding, immobilizing the injury, and preparing the patient for transport to a medical facility. In the case of a disease outbreak, protocols might include identifying and isolating the infected individuals, implementing quarantine measures, and providing supportive care while monitoring the spread of the disease.

In addition to physical injuries, communities must also be prepared to respond to psychological emergencies, which can arise in the aftermath of traumatic events. The mental health of community members is as important as their physical health, and protocols should include steps for providing emotional support, identifying individuals who may be at risk for mental health issues, and connecting them with appropriate resources or counseling. First responders should be trained to recognize the signs of psychological distress and to approach these situations with empathy and care, helping to prevent the long-term psychological impact of trauma.

Creating and maintaining emergency medical supplies is another vital component of the response system. A well-stocked first aid kit should be available in key locations throughout the community, such as at the health clinic, communal gathering areas, and in the homes of trained first responders. These kits should include essentials such as bandages, antiseptics, pain relievers, splints, and emergency blankets, as well as any specialized items needed for specific conditions or common injuries in the area. Communities should also establish a system for regularly checking and replenishing these supplies to ensure that they are always ready for use.

Moreover, transportation is a critical aspect of emergency medical response, particularly in situations where advanced care is needed beyond what first responders can provide. In a post-collapse world, where motorized vehicles may be scarce or unreliable, communities must develop alternative methods for transporting patients to medical facilities or other safe locations. This might include the use of carts, stretchers, or even makeshift litters that can be carried by multiple people. The community should also plan for the construction of safe and accessible routes to and from key locations, ensuring that patients can be transported quickly and safely in an emergency.

In conclusion, building an effective emergency medical response system is essential for the survival of a community in a post-collapse world. By training first responders, organizing a response network, developing emergency protocols, and ensuring the availability of medical supplies and transportation, communities can be better prepared to handle medical emergencies and reduce the impact of health crises. This preparedness not only saves lives but also enhances the overall resilience of the community, ensuring that it can weather the challenges of a world where professional medical care is no longer readily available.

Chapter 10: Education and Knowledge Preservation

Knowledge is a powerful force, and education is fundamental to the process of rebuilding civilization. This chapter highlights the critical importance of preserving and passing on knowledge, particularly through practical skills, science, and technology. By doing so, you can ensure your community is prepared for the future, equipping it with the tools necessary to adapt, innovate, and thrive in a changing world.

10.1 Establishing a Learning Environment

In the aftermath of societal collapse, the significance of education becomes even more critical. As communities embark on the challenging task of rebuilding, the preservation and transmission of knowledge are essential to ensure that the hard-earned lessons of the past are not forgotten and that future generations are equipped with the skills needed to thrive. Establishing a learning environment is the first step toward reviving education in a world where traditional schools and institutions may no longer exist. This process involves creating makeshift classrooms, recruiting educators and skilled community members, and developing a curriculum focused on survival, rebuilding, and the long-term success of the community.

Creating makeshift classrooms is a practical solution when formal educational spaces are unavailable. These classrooms need not be elaborate; they can be set up in any available shelter, such as a community center, a large room in a communal building, or even outdoors under a sturdy canopy. The most important factor is creating a dedicated space where learning can happen consistently and without distractions. This space should be arranged in a way that encourages focus and participation, with seating organized to facilitate interaction and group work. If possible, basic supplies like chalkboards, writing materials, and books should be gathered for students to use. In the absence of such materials, creative alternatives can be employed, such as using flat stones or wooden boards as slates, and charcoal or sharpened sticks as writing instruments.

Recruiting educators and knowledgeable community members is a key component of establishing a learning environment. In a post-collapse situation, the role of teachers may need to be redefined. Educators could be anyone within the community who has valuable knowledge or skills, regardless of formal teaching experience. These individuals could include former teachers, tradespeople, farmers, or elders with a wealth of traditional knowledge. The aim is to tap into the collective wisdom of the community to educate younger generations and impart the essential skills necessary for survival and rebuilding. These educators should be encouraged not only to share their expertise but also to ignite a passion for learning and creativity, fostering a culture of curiosity and resilience among the community members.

Designing a curriculum that focuses on survival and rebuilding is essential for making education relevant to the community's immediate needs. The curriculum should go beyond traditional academic subjects to include practical, hands-on skills critical for daily survival in a world without modern conveniences. While subjects like basic literacy and numeracy remain important, they should be integrated with lessons on topics such as farming, food preservation, construction, and basic healthcare. The curriculum should also include lessons on leadership, ethics, and community building, preparing students not only for survival but also for active roles in the governance and growth of the community. Flexibility is key, as the curriculum will need to adapt over time to address new challenges and emerging needs.

To provide a well-rounded education, it's important to balance practical skills with opportunities for creative and critical thinking. This can be achieved by incorporating storytelling, arts, and music into the curriculum, which helps preserve the community's cultural heritage while also offering students a chance to express themselves and explore new ideas. Encouraging students to ask questions, observe their surroundings, and develop innovative solutions will help them build the critical thinking and problem-solving skills necessary for navigating a rapidly changing world. By creating a learning environment that values both practical skills and intellectual exploration, the community can equip its members with the knowledge and mindset necessary to rebuild and thrive in the long term.

10.2 Teaching Practical Skills

In a world where the conveniences of modern life have disappeared, teaching practical skills becomes a cornerstone of education. These skills are not just useful—they are essential for survival and the successful rebuilding of the community. Prioritizing the teaching of essential survival skills, incorporating hands-on learning, and encouraging problem-solving and innovation are critical steps in creating a resilient and self-sufficient population. The focus of education must shift from abstract knowledge to practical application, ensuring that every member of the community, regardless of age, is equipped to contribute to the collective effort of survival and reconstruction.

The first priority in this new educational paradigm is to teach essential survival skills. These include farming, foraging, hunting, and fishing, which are necessary for food security. Understanding how to cultivate crops, raise livestock, and preserve food through methods such as drying, salting, and canning will ensure that the community can sustain itself even in the face of adversity. Construction skills, such as building shelters, making tools, and maintaining infrastructure, are also crucial. These skills not only provide the physical means to rebuild but also empower individuals with the knowledge to repair and innovate as needed. Additionally, basic healthcare skills—such as first aid, wound care, and the use of herbal remedies—are vital in a context where access to modern medicine may be limited. These skills ensure that minor injuries and illnesses do not escalate into life-threatening conditions.

Incorporating hands-on learning is key to effectively teaching these practical skills. Unlike traditional classroom settings where students might learn from textbooks and lectures, the new educational approach must emphasize learning by doing. For example, rather than merely teaching students about farming techniques in theory, they should be taken to the fields to plant, tend, and harvest crops themselves. Similarly, lessons on construction should involve actual building projects, such as constructing a new shelter or repairing community infrastructure. This approach not only reinforces the knowledge being taught but also allows students to develop the muscle memory and confidence needed to perform these tasks independently. Hands-on learning also fosters a deeper connection between the students and their environment, helping them to understand the practical implications of their actions and decisions.

Encouraging problem-solving and innovation is another critical component of teaching practical skills. In a world where resources are limited and challenges are constant, the ability to think creatively and adapt to new situations is invaluable. Educators should create opportunities for students to tackle real-world problems, whether it's finding a way to improve crop yields, designing more efficient tools, or developing new methods for water purification. These challenges not only teach practical skills but also promote a mindset of resilience and resourcefulness. Students should be encouraged to experiment, make mistakes, and learn from those experiences, as this process is essential for developing the ability to innovate and adapt in the face of uncertainty.

Moreover, teaching practical skills should be a community-wide effort, not confined to the young or to formal educational settings. All members of the community, regardless of age, should be involved in the learning process. This might include intergenerational learning, where elders pass down traditional knowledge and skills to younger members, or communal workshops where everyone can learn new techniques together. This inclusive approach ensures that knowledge is widely distributed and that everyone has the opportunity to contribute to the community's survival and rebuilding efforts.

The focus on practical skills does not mean abandoning intellectual or creative pursuits. Instead, these skills should be integrated into a broader educational framework that also values critical thinking, creativity, and cultural preservation. For instance, students learning about agriculture might also study the science behind soil health and crop rotation, or those learning construction might explore the principles of engineering and architecture. By blending practical skills with intellectual inquiry, the community can foster a well-rounded education that prepares individuals to not only survive but to rebuild a thriving, sustainable society.

In summary, teaching practical skills is an essential part of education in a post-collapse world. By prioritizing survival skills, incorporating hands-on learning, and encouraging problem-solving and innovation, communities can equip their members with the tools they need to rebuild and thrive. This approach not only ensures that the community can meet its immediate needs but also lays the foundation for long-term resilience and self-sufficiency, empowering individuals to take an active role in the ongoing effort to rebuild and improve their world.

10.3 Science and Technology for the Future

In the wake of a societal collapse, the preservation and advancement of science and technology become crucial for the long-term survival and growth of any community. While the immediate focus may be on survival and rebuilding basic infrastructure, it is essential not to lose sight of the role that science and technology play in shaping a sustainable and resilient future. Understanding and applying the basic principles of science and engineering, encouraging experimentation and technological adaptation, and working toward the reconstruction of essential technological infrastructure are key steps in ensuring that communities can not only survive but also thrive in the post-collapse world.

The foundation of science and technology education in a post-collapse environment lies in teaching the basic principles of science and engineering. Even in the absence of advanced tools and laboratories, these principles can be conveyed through simple, practical experiments and observations that demonstrate the underlying concepts. For example, lessons on physics can be taught by exploring basic mechanics through the construction of simple machines like levers and pulleys, which can then be applied to real-world tasks such as lifting heavy objects or constructing buildings. Chemistry can be introduced through the creation of rudimentary batteries or the fermentation process, demonstrating how chemical reactions can be harnessed for energy and food preservation. Biology lessons might focus on understanding ecosystems, the principles of sustainable agriculture, or the basics of human anatomy and health.

By grounding scientific education in practical, hands-on experiences, communities can ensure that their members develop a functional understanding of these concepts and are able to apply them in their daily lives. This approach not only helps preserve scientific knowledge but also empowers individuals to think critically and solve problems using the resources available to them. In this way, science education becomes directly relevant to the community's survival and development, rather than being seen as an abstract or distant field of study.

Encouraging experimentation and technological adaptation is another crucial element of science and technology education. In a world where the technological landscape has drastically changed, communities must be able to adapt existing technologies to new circumstances or develop entirely new solutions to meet their needs. This requires a mindset of curiosity and innovation, where experimentation is encouraged and failure is seen as a learning opportunity rather than a setback. Communities should foster a culture of tinkering and problem-solving, where individuals feel empowered to modify tools, invent new devices, or repurpose materials in creative ways.

For example, the community might experiment with alternative energy sources, such as designing small-scale wind turbines or solar collectors using scavenged materials. They could explore ways to improve agricultural productivity through the development of simple irrigation systems or experiment with new methods of food preservation that extend the shelf life of perishable goods. By encouraging these kinds of projects, the community not only develops practical solutions to immediate challenges but also builds a base of technological knowledge that can be expanded upon as resources and capabilities grow.

It is also important to recognize that science and technology education should not be limited to those with a formal background in these fields. In a post-collapse world, every member of the community can contribute to the advancement of technology through their unique experiences and perspectives. Farmers, builders, and artisans all possess valuable knowledge that can be integrated into scientific and technological endeavors. This inclusive approach ensures that the community's efforts are grounded in practical reality and that innovations are accessible and relevant to everyone.

Rebuilding essential technological infrastructure is the ultimate goal of science and technology education in a post-collapse scenario. While it may not be possible to immediately restore all the conveniences of modern life, communities can work toward reestablishing key technologies that enhance their quality of life and support their long-term sustainability. This might include the construction of basic communication systems, such as radio networks that allow for coordination with neighboring communities, or the development of water purification systems that ensure a safe and reliable supply of drinking water. In the realm of agriculture, the community could focus on developing more efficient tools for planting and harvesting crops or constructing greenhouses that extend the growing season.

The reconstruction of technological infrastructure should be approached with an eye toward sustainability and resilience. Rather than simply trying to replicate the technologies of the pre-collapse world, communities should consider how these systems can be improved to better suit the current environment. This might involve using renewable energy sources, designing technologies that are easily repairable with available materials, or developing systems that are scalable and adaptable to different conditions. By taking this approach, communities not only rebuild their technological capabilities but also ensure that these systems are robust and capable of evolving over time.

Furthermore, science and technology education can play a critical role in fostering a sense of hope and progress within the community. In a world where the future is uncertain, the ability to innovate and create new technologies can provide a sense of agency and control. It reminds the community that, despite the challenges they face, they have the power to shape their own destiny and improve their circumstances through knowledge and ingenuity. This forward-looking perspective is essential for maintaining morale and motivation, as it reinforces the idea that the community is not merely surviving but actively working toward a better future.

In conclusion, science and technology are integral to the long-term success of any community in a post-collapse world. By teaching the basic principles of science and engineering, encouraging experimentation and technological adaptation, and focusing on the reconstruction of essential technological infrastructure, communities can build a foundation for sustainable growth and resilience. This approach not only preserves valuable knowledge but also empowers individuals to take an active role in rebuilding and improving their world, ensuring that the community is well-equipped to face the challenges of the future.

Chapter 11: Reconnecting with Nature

Nature serves as both a provider and a protector. In this chapter, you will explore how to restore natural ecosystems, implement sustainable agricultural practices, and prepare for environmental challenges. These efforts are crucial for establishing a harmonious and mutually beneficial relationship with the environment, ensuring the long-term resilience of both the land and the community. By understanding how to work with nature rather than against it, communities can create a sustainable future that respects natural resources while promoting ecological health.

11.1 Restoring Natural Ecosystems

In a post-collapse world, it is essential to redefine and nurture the relationship between humans and the natural environment. Restoring natural ecosystems plays a central role in this process, as healthy ecosystems form the foundation for sustainable community rebuilding. A thriving environment not only provides vital resources like clean water, fertile soil, and food but also offers protection against natural disasters and climate extremes. Engaging in activities such as reforestation, habitat restoration, and protecting local wildlife and biodiversity are critical steps to repairing the damage caused by human activity and ensuring that the environment can sustain future generations.

Reforestation is one of the most effective strategies to restore natural ecosystems. Forests are crucial for maintaining the planet's overall health, helping regulate the climate, stabilize soil, and provide habitats for countless species. In many regions, deforestation has left land barren and exposed to erosion, flooding, and biodiversity loss. By planting trees and restoring forests, communities can begin to undo some of this damage. This process goes beyond simply planting trees; it requires careful planning to ensure that the appropriate species are selected for the ecosystem, that they are planted in a way that reflects natural growth patterns, and that the forest is allowed to regenerate naturally over time. Reforestation efforts should focus on native species that are well-suited to the local environment, as these plants are more resilient and provide better support for local wildlife.

Habitat restoration works in tandem with reforestation, involving the rehabilitation of entire ecosystems, including wetlands, grasslands, and coastal areas. These ecosystems are often overlooked, but they are just as critical as forests in maintaining ecological balance. Wetlands, for example, serve as natural water filtration systems and flood buffers, while coastal ecosystems like mangroves protect against storm surges and coastal erosion. Restoring these habitats includes removing invasive species, reintroducing native plants and animals, and in some cases, re-engineering the landscape to restore natural water flows or soil conditions. The goal is to create a self-sustaining ecosystem that can support a diverse range of species and provide valuable ecosystem services to the community.

Protecting local wildlife and biodiversity is another key element of restoring natural ecosystems. Biodiversity is the web of life that supports the health of the planet; it provides ecosystem resilience, genetic resources for food and medicine, and cultural and recreational benefits. In a post-collapse world, where many species may be threatened by habitat loss, pollution, and climate change, it is crucial to actively protect and preserve local wildlife. This can include creating wildlife corridors to connect fragmented habitats, establishing protected areas where hunting and development are prohibited, and implementing species recovery programs for endangered plants and animals. Communities should also be educated about the importance of biodiversity and learn how to coexist with local wildlife, minimizing conflicts and avoiding harmful chemicals that can poison the environment.

Sustainable hunting and fishing practices are essential for maintaining the balance of natural ecosystems. In many traditional societies, hunting and fishing are integral to culture and economy. However, without proper management, these practices can lead to overexploitation and the collapse of wildlife populations. Sustainable practices include setting limits on the number of animals hunted or fish caught, ensuring that only certain species are targeted while others are protected, and employing methods that minimize environmental harm. For instance, selective fishing techniques can reduce bycatch, and community-managed hunting zones can help maintain healthy and sustainable wildlife populations. By adopting these practices, communities can continue benefiting from natural resources without undermining ecosystem health.

In conclusion, restoring natural ecosystems is a complex, multi-faceted effort that involves reforestation, habitat restoration, wildlife protection, and sustainable resource management. These actions not only heal the land but also foster a harmonious relationship between humans and nature, supporting both ecological and human health for future generations. By prioritizing the restoration and protection of natural ecosystems, communities can lay the groundwork for a resilient, self-sustaining future.

11.2 Sustainable Agriculture and Permaculture

As communities seek to reconnect with nature in the aftermath of societal collapse, sustainable agriculture and permaculture practices offer a way to produce food that is not only efficient but also harmonious with the environment. Unlike conventional farming, which often relies on monocultures, chemical fertilizers, and pesticides, sustainable agriculture and permaculture focus on creating agricultural systems that mimic the complexity and resilience of natural ecosystems. This approach not only improves soil health and increases biodiversity but also reduces the need for external inputs, making the community more self-reliant and environmentally friendly.

Permaculture is a design philosophy that seeks to create self-sustaining agricultural systems by integrating plants, animals, and people in ways that are mutually beneficial. At its core, permaculture is about observing and mimicking the patterns found in nature to create agricultural systems that are resilient, sustainable, and productive. For example, instead of planting a single crop in a large field, a permaculture garden might include a diverse mix of plants that support each other in various ways—some fixing nitrogen in the soil, others attracting pollinators, and still others providing ground cover to retain moisture and prevent erosion. This diversity not only makes the system more resilient to pests and diseases but also ensures that it can continue to produce food year after year without depleting the soil.

One of the key principles of permaculture is the integration of animals and plants into a sustainable cycle. Animals play an essential role in maintaining the health of a permaculture system by providing manure, which enriches the soil, and by controlling pests. For example, chickens can be used to clear fields of weeds and insects while simultaneously fertilizing the soil with their droppings. Similarly, ducks can be introduced into rice paddies to eat pests and aerate the water, reducing the need for chemical pesticides and fertilizers. By integrating animals into the farming system in a way that mimics their natural roles, permaculture not only increases the efficiency of food production but also creates a more balanced and sustainable ecosystem.

Creating food forests is another powerful technique used in permaculture to develop sustainable gardens. A food forest is a multi-layered garden that mimics a natural forest, with different plants occupying different levels or "strata." This includes tall fruit and nut trees forming the canopy, smaller trees and shrubs in the understory, herbs and vegetables at ground level, and root crops underground. The diverse plant species in a food forest work together to create a stable and productive ecosystem that requires minimal maintenance. The trees provide shade and reduce the need for irrigation, the shrubs attract beneficial insects, and the ground cover helps retain moisture and prevent weeds. Over time, a well-designed food forest can produce a wide variety of fruits, nuts, vegetables, and herbs with little or no need for artificial inputs.

In addition to food forests, sustainable gardens can take many forms, depending on the needs and resources of the community. Raised bed gardens, for example, are an excellent option in areas with poor soil or limited space, as they allow for better control over soil quality and drainage. Companion planting—growing certain plants together because they benefit each other—can also enhance productivity and reduce the need for chemical inputs. For instance, planting marigolds alongside tomatoes can help deter pests, while beans planted with corn can fix nitrogen in the soil, benefiting both crops. By incorporating these sustainable practices, communities can create gardens that are not only productive but also ecologically sound.

Moreover, sustainable agriculture and permaculture are not just about growing food; they are also about building a deeper connection between people and the land. These practices encourage communities to work with nature rather than against it, fostering a sense of stewardship and respect for the environment. They also promote self-reliance, as communities learn to produce their own food in a way that is both sustainable and resilient to environmental challenges. In a post-collapse world, where external resources may be scarce or unreliable, the ability to produce food sustainably is crucial for long-term survival.

In conclusion, sustainable agriculture and permaculture offer a holistic approach to food production that integrates the principles of ecology with the practical needs of the community. By designing agricultural systems that mimic natural ecosystems, integrating animals and plants into sustainable cycles, and creating food forests and sustainable gardens, communities can ensure a steady supply of food while also protecting and enhancing the environment. These practices not only provide immediate benefits in terms of food security but also contribute to the long-term resilience and sustainability of the community as a whole.

11.3 Preparing for Environmental Challenges

In a post-collapse world, the ability to anticipate and respond to environmental challenges is critical for the survival and resilience of any community. As the global climate continues to change, and as natural disasters become more frequent and severe, communities must develop strategies to mitigate these risks and adapt to new environmental realities. Preparing for environmental challenges involves a deep understanding of climate-related risks, proactive planning for natural disasters and extreme weather, and fostering community resilience to environmental changes. By taking these steps, communities can protect themselves against the unpredictable forces of nature and ensure their long-term sustainability.

Understanding and mitigating climate-related risks is the first step in preparing for environmental challenges. Climate change has led to an increase in the frequency and intensity of extreme weather events, such as hurricanes, floods, droughts, and wildfires. These events can have devastating effects on communities, particularly those that are already vulnerable due to limited resources or geographic location. To effectively prepare for these risks, communities must first conduct a thorough assessment of their local environment, identifying the specific threats they are most likely to face. This might involve studying historical weather patterns, monitoring changes in local ecosystems, and consulting with experts or other communities that have faced similar challenges.

Once the risks have been identified, the next step is to develop strategies for mitigating them. This might include building infrastructure that is resilient to extreme weather, such as flood barriers, wind-resistant shelters, or firebreaks. For example, in areas prone to flooding, communities might construct levees, create retention ponds, or restore wetlands to absorb excess water. In regions at risk of wildfires, clearing brush and creating firebreaks can help prevent the spread of fires, while building homes with fire-resistant materials can reduce the damage if a fire does occur. Communities should also consider the long-term impacts of climate change, such as rising sea levels or changing precipitation patterns, and plan accordingly. This might involve relocating vulnerable populations, diversifying water sources, or transitioning to crops that are better suited to the new climate conditions.

Preparing for natural disasters and extreme weather is another critical aspect of environmental resilience. In a post-collapse world, where external assistance may be unavailable or delayed, communities must be self-reliant in responding to emergencies. This requires the development of comprehensive disaster preparedness plans that include clear protocols for evacuation, emergency communication, and the distribution of supplies. These plans should be regularly reviewed and updated to reflect new information or changes in the environment. Drills and simulations are also essential for ensuring that all community members know how to respond in an emergency. For example, practicing evacuation routes, setting up temporary shelters, and conducting search and rescue exercises can help build confidence and coordination among community members.

In addition to physical preparations, communities should also invest in building social resilience to environmental challenges. This involves fostering strong social networks, promoting cooperation, and ensuring that all members of the community have access to the resources and support they need to recover from disasters. In the aftermath of a natural disaster, social cohesion can make a significant difference in the speed and effectiveness of recovery efforts. Communities that are united, where members trust and support one another, are better able to pool resources, share information, and rebuild together. This social resilience is just as important as physical resilience in ensuring the long-term survival of the community.

Developing community resilience to environmental changes also requires a proactive approach to adaptation. As the environment changes, communities must be willing to adapt their practices, technologies, and lifestyles to the new conditions. This might involve transitioning to more sustainable agricultural practices that are better suited to the changing climate, such as drought-resistant crops or agroforestry systems that enhance soil moisture and reduce the need for irrigation. It could also involve adopting new technologies, such as rainwater harvesting systems or solar-powered desalination plants, to ensure a reliable supply of clean water in regions where traditional water sources are becoming scarce. Communities should also consider the impact of climate change on local biodiversity and take steps to protect and restore ecosystems that provide essential services, such as pollination, water filtration, and carbon sequestration.

Education and awareness are key components of building resilience to environmental challenges. Community members need to be informed about the risks they face and the steps they can take to protect themselves and their environment. This might involve workshops, training sessions, or public information campaigns that teach people how to prepare for natural disasters, reduce their environmental footprint, and adapt to changing conditions. It is also important to involve the community in the decision-making process, ensuring that everyone has a voice in shaping the strategies and policies that will affect their future. By fostering a culture of environmental awareness and stewardship, communities can build a strong foundation for resilience that will serve them well in the face of future challenges.

Conclusion: The Path Forward: Building a Thriving and Resilient Future

Reflecting on the Journey

As we reach the conclusion of this comprehensive guide, it is important to pause and reflect on the journey we have undertaken together. This journey has not only been about acquiring the necessary knowledge and skills to survive and rebuild in a post-collapse world, but also about understanding the deeper principles that underpin the creation of a thriving, resilient society. Across the ten chapters, we have explored critical aspects of survival, sustainability, governance, and community-building—each of which is integral to forming a new civilization that is stronger, more sustainable, and more just than the one that came before.

In the first chapter, we laid the foundation for survival in the immediate aftermath of societal collapse. We began by analyzing the common causes of collapses, recognizing signs that signal an impending breakdown, and examining the psychological impact on both individuals and communities. Our focus then shifted to survival essentials: securing water sources, constructing or finding shelter, and ensuring a sufficient food supply. We also highlighted the importance of self-defense and security in a world where traditional law enforcement may no longer be reliable and discussed the importance of basic medical preparedness, including first aid skills and the creation of a medical kit. The chapter concluded with the emphasis on forming a survival group, stressing that community is vital for survival.

The second chapter focused on creating a sustainable food supply, a critical element for long-term survival. We discussed gardening for survival, choosing crops that thrive in various climates, and using techniques to maximize yield with minimal resources. We explored foraging and hunting as supplementary food sources, emphasizing the importance of identifying edible wild plants and basic hunting and trapping techniques. Animal husbandry was introduced as a means of ensuring a stable food source, providing guidance on selecting the right livestock and constructing and maintaining their shelters. Lastly, we covered various food preservation methods, such as canning, pickling, dehydration, and root cellaring, to ensure the longevity of food supplies during hard times.

Chapter three was dedicated to building and maintaining shelter, one of the most fundamental aspects of survival. We began with strategic considerations for selecting a safe location, assessing natural resources, and zoning a community for optimal functionality. We introduced basic construction techniques, offering practical advice on building sturdy, weather-resistant structures using available materials. The chapter also explored advanced building techniques, including the use of sustainable materials like earthbags, cob, and straw bales, and integrating renewable energy sources. The importance of ongoing maintenance and repairs was emphasized to ensure the longevity of shelters, along with creating living spaces that promote comfort and mental well-being.

Water management and sanitation were the focus of chapter four, recognizing that access to clean water and proper waste management is essential to preventing disease and maintaining community health. We discussed methods for finding and purifying water, including locating water sources in the wild and setting up rainwater collection systems. The chapter explored building water systems, including wells, cisterns, and gravity-fed systems, along with irrigation techniques to support sustainable agriculture. Waste management systems such as composting toilets and greywater solutions were also covered as key components of a healthy community. The chapter concluded with the importance of community water infrastructure, including equitable distribution and managing shared water resources.

Chapter five addressed the reconstruction of communication and transportation networks, crucial for connecting isolated communities and facilitating the flow of goods and information. We began with emergency communication systems, including basic radio operation, local communication networks, and using non-verbal methods such as Morse code. The chapter then shifted to rebuilding transportation systems, with advice on clearing and maintaining roads, adopting alternative transportation methods, and setting up a community transport system. Signaling for help, a vital skill in emergencies, was also discussed, including creating effective visual and auditory signals. The chapter concluded by exploring long-distance travel and exploration, focusing on navigation skills and the creation of simple maps.

In chapter six, we explored energy solutions, recognizing that access to power is crucial for maintaining a functioning community. We discussed the potential of solar energy, covering the construction and upkeep of solar panels, solar water heaters, and solar cookers. Wind and water power were introduced as alternative energy sources, with guidance on building wind turbines, water wheels, and micro-hydro systems. The chapter also covered bioenergy, including biofuels and biogas digesters, and highlighted energy storage solutions, such as battery systems and thermal mass storage. We wrapped up with energy conservation strategies to reduce energy needs and promote sustainability.

Chapter seven shifted focus to social structures, beginning with the establishment of leadership. We discussed identifying natural leaders, creating a governance council, and developing inclusive decision-making processes. The creation of laws and regulations was explored, focusing on establishing a code of conduct and ensuring fair enforcement as the community evolves. We also covered the importance of fostering a resilient culture, emphasizing cooperation, sustainability, and the promotion of arts and literature that reflect the new society.

In chapter eight, we addressed health and medicine in a world where modern healthcare may be limited. We began by outlining the establishment of a community health system, including training healthcare providers, setting up clinics, and creating a medical supply chain. The chapter also explored traditional and herbal medicine as valuable resources, as well as the importance of preventive healthcare, sanitation, and hygiene. Emergency medical response was another focus, with advice on preparing for common medical emergencies, building a network of first responders, and developing protocols for disease outbreaks.

Chapter nine focused on education and knowledge preservation, underscoring the importance of transmitting knowledge for the future. We explored establishing makeshift classrooms, recruiting educators, and creating a curriculum that emphasizes survival and rebuilding. Practical skills such as farming, construction, and problem-solving were emphasized, as well as the role of science and technology in the future. Encouraging experimentation and technological adaptation was also discussed, along with the need to reconstruct essential technological infrastructure.

In the final chapter, chapter ten, we examined the importance of reconnecting with nature as a foundation for sustainable living. We explored the restoration of natural ecosystems through reforestation, habitat restoration, and the protection of local wildlife and biodiversity. Sustainable agriculture and permaculture practices were highlighted as crucial for creating food systems in harmony with nature. The chapter concluded with advice on preparing for environmental challenges, including climate-related risks, natural disaster preparedness, and building community resilience to environmental changes..

The Importance of Community

Throughout this journey, one theme has remained constant: the importance of community. Rebuilding civilization is not an individual endeavor; it is a collective effort that requires the collaboration, support, and mutual aid of every member of the community. The challenges of a post-collapse world are too great for any one person to overcome alone, and it is through the strength of community that we find the resilience and resources needed to rebuild.

In each chapter, we have seen how the involvement of the community is crucial to success. Whether it is forming a survival group in the immediate aftermath of a collapse, establishing a sustainable food supply, building and maintaining shelter, or reestablishing communication and transportation networks, the collective effort of the community is what makes these endeavors possible. Community members bring diverse skills, knowledge, and perspectives, and when these are pooled together, they create a powerful force for survival and progress.

Community is also the foundation of social structures, governance, and culture. As we discussed in chapter seven, establishing leadership and creating laws requires the participation and support of the entire community. Building a resilient culture, promoting values of cooperation and sustainability, and fostering the arts and literature that reflect the new society are all efforts that depend on the active engagement of the community. It is through these shared endeavors that a sense of solidarity and belonging is created, which is essential for the long-term stability and prosperity of the community.

In the realm of health and medicine, the community plays a vital role in maintaining health and preventing disease. The establishment of a community health system, the practice of traditional and herbal medicine, and the promotion of preventive healthcare and hygiene all rely on the collective effort of the community. In times of emergency, it is the community that comes together to provide care, support, and resources to those in need.

Education and knowledge preservation are also deeply rooted in the community. As we discussed in chapter nine, the transmission of knowledge is a collective responsibility. Educators, parents, elders, and community members all contribute to the education of the younger generation, ensuring that essential skills, knowledge, and values are passed down. Science and technology, too, are advanced through the collaborative efforts of the community, as individuals share their expertise, experiment with new ideas, and work together to rebuild technological infrastructure.

Finally, in reconnecting with nature, the community plays a central role in restoring natural ecosystems, practicing sustainable agriculture, and preparing for environmental challenges. These efforts require the participation of every member of the community, as the health of the environment is directly linked to the well-being of the community. By working together to protect and restore the natural world, communities can create a sustainable future for themselves and future generations.

The importance of community cannot be overstated. It is through the strength of community that we find the resilience, resources, and support needed to rebuild civilization. Rebuilding civilization is not just about surviving; it is about thriving, and this is only possible when we work together, support one another, and build a society based on the principles of cooperation, mutual aid, and shared responsibility.

Looking to the Future

As we look to the future, we envision a new society built on the principles of sustainability, resilience, and cooperation. This new society is not a return to the old ways but a reimagining of what civilization can be. It is a society that learns from the mistakes of the past, that values the health of the planet as much as the health of its people, and that prioritizes the well-being of the community over individual gain.

In this new society, sustainability is at the core of every decision. The lessons learned from the collapse teach us that the unchecked exploitation of resources, the disregard for the environment, and the focus on short-term profits over long-term sustainability are paths to disaster. In the new society, sustainable practices are not just encouraged; they are essential. Whether it is in agriculture, energy production, construction, or governance, every decision is made with the understanding that the future of the community depends on the health of the environment.

Resilience is another key principle of the new society. The collapse has shown us that the systems we once relied on are fragile and vulnerable to disruption. In the new society, resilience is built into every aspect of life. This means creating systems that are flexible, adaptable, and capable of withstanding shocks and stresses. It means fostering a culture of innovation and problem-solving, where challenges are seen as opportunities to grow and improve. It also means building strong social networks and a sense of community that can provide support in times of crisis.

Cooperation is the third pillar of the new society. The collapse has taught us that we are stronger together than we are alone. In the new society, cooperation is not just a strategy; it is a value that is deeply ingrained in the culture. Whether it is working together to produce food, build shelter, or protect the environment, cooperation is seen as the key to success. This spirit of cooperation extends beyond the boundaries of individual communities, fostering collaboration and mutual support between different groups and regions.

As a reader, you have played a crucial role in this journey. By engaging with the content of this book, you have taken the first steps toward becoming a leader, a teacher, and a builder of the new society. The knowledge and skills you have acquired are not just tools for survival; they are the building blocks of a better future. You have the power to shape this future, to influence the direction of your community, and to contribute to the creation of a society that is more just, more sustainable, and more resilient than the one that came before.

Your role in shaping this future is not limited to your actions in the present. As you continue to learn, grow, and adapt, you will become a source of knowledge and inspiration for others. You will have the opportunity to teach, to lead, and to mentor the next generation of builders and thinkers. Your experiences, your successes, and even your failures will contribute to the collective wisdom of the community, helping to guide future decisions and actions.

In looking to the future, it is important to remember that the journey of rebuilding civilization is not a linear path. There will be setbacks, challenges, and moments of doubt. But it is in these moments that the true strength of the community will be revealed. By staying committed to the principles of sustainability, resilience, and cooperation, and by supporting one another through the ups and downs, the community can overcome any obstacle and continue to move forward.

As we envision this new society, it is also important to recognize that the work of rebuilding is never truly complete. The world is constantly changing, and the challenges of today will not be the challenges of tomorrow. The new society must be dynamic, capable of evolving and adapting to new circumstances. This requires a mindset of continuous learning and improvement, where every member of the community is encouraged to contribute ideas, to experiment, and to innovate. It also requires a commitment to inclusivity, ensuring that all voices are heard, and that everyone has a role to play in shaping the future.

In conclusion, looking to the future is about more than just survival; it is about creating a world that reflects the best of what humanity can achieve. It is about building a society that is sustainable, resilient, and cooperative, where the health of the planet and the well-being of the community are at the forefront of every decision. As a reader, you have the knowledge, the skills, and the power to shape this future. The journey may be challenging, but it is also filled with opportunities to create something truly extraordinary. Together, we can build a world that is not only capable of surviving but also of thriving for generations to come.

Final Words of Encouragement

As we conclude this journey, it is important to leave you with a sense of hope, purpose, and empowerment. The task of rebuilding civilization is monumental, but it is not insurmountable. Throughout history, humanity has faced countless challenges, and time and again, we have risen to the occasion. The resilience, creativity, and determination that have carried us through the darkest of times are the same qualities that will guide us as we rebuild.

The power of individual and collective action cannot be overstated. Every action you take, no matter how small, contributes to the greater goal of rebuilding civilization. Whether you are planting a garden, teaching a child, constructing a shelter, or leading a community, your efforts matter. You are part of a larger movement, a global effort to create a better, more sustainable world. And as you take these actions, you inspire others to do the same, creating a ripple effect that spreads far beyond your immediate surroundings.

Remember that you are not alone on this journey. The challenges you face are shared by communities around the world, and the solutions you develop can inspire and support others. Collaboration and mutual support are key to overcoming the obstacles ahead. By working together, sharing knowledge, and learning from one another, we can achieve far more than we ever could alone.

As you move forward, it is important to stay focused on the principles that have guided this journey: sustainability, resilience, and cooperation. These principles are not just ideals; they are the foundation upon which the new society will be built. They are the keys to creating a world that is capable of withstanding the challenges of the future and providing a safe, healthy, and fulfilling life for all its members.

In the face of adversity, it is easy to become discouraged, to feel overwhelmed by the enormity of the task ahead. But it is in these moments that you must hold on to hope and remember that every step forward, no matter how small, brings us closer to the world we envision. The journey of rebuilding civilization is not a sprint; it is a marathon, and it is one that we must undertake with patience, perseverance, and a steadfast commitment to our goals.

As you continue on this path, take pride in the progress you have made and the contributions you have given. Celebrate your successes, learn from your failures, and keep moving forward with determination and purpose. The road ahead may be long, but it is also filled with opportunities to create a better world, a world that reflects the best of what humanity can achieve.

In the end, the journey of rebuilding civilization is about more than just survival; it is about creating a legacy for future generations. It is about ensuring that the mistakes of the past are not repeated and that the world we leave behind is one of peace, prosperity, and harmony with the natural world. This is a journey that requires courage, vision, and unwavering commitment, but it is one that is worth undertaking.

So as we close this book, know that the power to shape the future is in your hands. You have the knowledge, the skills, and the determination to make a difference. The journey may be challenging, but it is also filled with potential. Together, we can build a world that is not only capable of surviving but also of thriving for generations to come. The future is yours to create, and it starts with the actions you take today.

Thank you!

We have come to the end of a challenging yet rewarding journey together. Your commitment to delving into the depths of survival strategies, sustainable living practices, and the principles of rebuilding civilization is truly commendable. This book is a reflection of not just my knowledge and experience, but also your dedication to learning and growing in the face of uncertainty.

If this guide has provided you with valuable insights and practical advice, I would be immensely grateful if you could share your thoughts through a review. Your feedback is not only appreciated but vital in helping others find the information they need to prepare for and thrive in any situation.

Thank you for taking this journey toward resilience and self-reliance. Your efforts to embrace these principles contribute to a more sustainable and hopeful future for all. Together, we can build a world that not only survives but flourishes in harmony with our surroundings.

www.ingramcontent.com/pod-product-compliance
Lightning Source LLC
Chambersburg PA
CBHW062225080426
42734CB00010B/2027